In The Cleft
Of The Rock

**Insights into the Blood of Jesus,
Resurrection Power, and Saving the Soul**

By Michael J. Webb

**Michael Webb
Today's Manna
www.todaysmanna.org
m&o@todaysmanna.org**

In The Cleft Of The Rock:
Insights into the Blood of Jesus, Resurrection Power, and Saving
the Soul
by Michael J. Webb

Printed in the United States of America

ISBN 978-1-60266-301-5

Scripture Quotations taken from Dake's Annotated Reference Bible, Authorized King James Version copyright © 1961, 1963, 1989, 1991, and The Complete Jewish Bible, ed. David Stern, copyright © 1998.

www.xulonpress.com

David —

Blessings,

JN 14:21

8/07

Table of Contents

—ɯ—

Preface

—〰—

We are living in what may be the most exciting time since Jesus first walked among men. We are also currently in the midst of the most radical transformation of the Body of Christ since the Reformation. If we are indeed in the season of His return, as many believe, we will witness, and participate in, events that not only have eternal significance, but will shake the foundations of modern Christianity.

The image of the Church as it appears in the minds of many today, both religious and secular, will not be the image of the Church in the near future.

Sadly, many in the Body of Christ are ill-prepared for events which will unfold in the Earth prior to the return of the Great King. The primary reason for this is that few Believers have an intimate relationship with Jesus. As John Calvin wrote, many are part of the "visible," or "professing," Church. They may know the Book of the Lord, but they do not know the Lord of the Book. They know *about* Jesus, but they do not truly *know* Him.

Jesus warned his Apostles—and through them, future generations of disciples—that many would come in His name, claiming relationship with Him, when, in fact, they would instead be wolves in sheep's clothing. Timothy warned that in the Last Days, many would have a form of godliness, but deny the power of God. And the Apostle Paul warned that all who desire to know the power of His resurrection, and the fellowship of His sufferings, must be wary of those who would preach "another gospel."

The Lord admonishes us directly about having a *laissez faire* attitude toward Him through the Apostle John in the Book of Revelation, saying, "I know your works, that you are neither hot nor cold: I wish that you were hot or cold. So then, because you are lukewarm, and neither cold nor hot, I will spew you out of my mouth." It is beyond frightening to think of the consequences of a lukewarm relationship with the Ancient of Days.

If we are going to truly be overcomers in the difficult days to come, we must develop an intimate relationship with God the Father through Jesus the Son. We must invite the Holy Spirit to transform our mind, will, and emotions so that we might become perfect, or complete, in Him. We must allow Jesus to become not only the Shepherd of our souls, but the Bishop as well.

Simply put, many have cried out and made Jesus their Savior, but have they allowed Him to become their Lord?

It has never been enough simply to "profess" Christ. If we sincerely desire to be salt and light in the midst of a dying world, we must do far more—we must "put on" Christ. That is, we must not forget for a moment that it is Christ "in us," Immanuel, Who is the only hope of glory; that it is only by, and through, Him that we defeat the enemy of our souls and walk victorious on a daily basis. One of the most encouraging promises Jesus gave us is this: even as He overcame the world, we too, through the power of the Holy Spirit, can overcome the world. Jesus did not ransom the keys of Hell and Death simply so we could "be saved," and then "go to Heaven." He held something far more significant in His heart as He hung on that bloody Cross and looked down through time.

He knew that, through the power of His Resurrection, He would become the "firstborn of many." A called-out group of people who would represent Him as faithful ambassadors on the Earth—living, walking, breathing examples of the Kingdom of God.

This book is the first in a series of three about the Glory of God, The Resurrected Church, and the coming Apostolic Move of the Holy Spirit. It has been in my heart for over a decade to share with the Body of Christ fresh perspectives on such topics as the Blood of Jesus, Resurrection Power, and the Saving of the Soul. I pray that as you read the following pages, the Holy Spirit will stir up a burning desire within you to search Scripture under His guidance, and that you will learn of the magnificent destiny God has prepared for all of those who diligently seek Him.

I also pray that, like the Shulamite woman in the Song of Songs, you will discover the "Lover of your soul" in the cleft of the rock.

Michael Webb
March 2007

For my parents, Jack and Mickie

Special thanks to Dr. Noel Fuller, and his wife, Pam,
for making the publication of this book possible.

Gethsemane

—w—

Have you ever been to Gethsemane?
Not the physical one. Rather, I'm speaking of the spiritual one.

How do you know if you've been?

Gethsemane is a place of great pain. It is also a place of death. Not physical death, but the death of the soul. For the most part, few in the Body of Christ have ever been to this place of spiritual confrontation. This is one of the main reasons so few Christians live the victorious life Scripture promises is available to us.

In Matthew 26:38 Jesus says, "My soul is exceedingly sorrowful, even unto death . . ." And Luke tells us in his account of the same event that Christ was in such agony that He was sweating great drops of blood. I don't know if you've ever really thought about what it must have been like for our Lord during his short time in the garden of Gethsemane on the eve of his crucifixion, but it seems clear from Scripture that a titanic struggle was taking place.

By all accounts in the Bible, Jesus never took three hours to accomplish any of His miracles, and yet we see Him in the garden struggling in agony for an extended period of time.

What on Earth was going on?

Most sermons preached on these passages focus on the fact that Jesus wrestled with the physical reality of the terrible necessity of the cross. While that is certainly one aspect of His tremendous travail, there is a much more fundamental principle being demonstrated here—one that goes to the very heart of the salvation experience.

In order for us to fully understand what our Lord was dealing with in the garden of Gethsemane, we must go back to the beginning. Back to another garden. The garden where humanity's entire struggle began.

Scripture teaches that man was created in the image and likeness of God, and that because of deception and disobedience humanity became estranged from its Creator. Eve was deceived, but Adam disobeyed. Thus, two distinctly different activities occurred resulting in one cumulative consequence.

Genesis 3:1 says, "Now the serpent was more subtle than any beast of the field which the Lord God had made." The Hebrew word for serpent is derived from the prime root *nahash,* meaning divination, enchantment, omen, or sorcery. The Hebrew word translated *"subtle"* literally means *"cunning,"* and is most often used in the negative sense. Hence, we have a deviously cunning enchanter, or sorcerer, deceiving Eve.

When God asks Eve what she has done, she responds by saying that the serpent beguiled her. The Hebrew word translated *"beguiled"* has the sense of both seduction and deception. Perhaps the serpent's power of deception was actually an enchantment, or a spell, which produced confusion in Eve's mind. At the same time, the serpent appealed to that aspect which is resident in all of us—pride. It was pride that caused Lucifer's fall from Heaven, and pride that ultimately led him to believe that he could not only become like the Most High God, but usurp His power and authority as well.

That old devil, the serpent—very possibly Lucifer in disguise— revealed himself in what he told Eve: "For God knows that in the day you eat, then your eyes shall be opened, and you shall be as gods, knowing good and evil." (Genesis 3:5) The enchanter evidently had a strong sense that this particular appeal to a desire to "be as a god" would be effective in obtaining what he wanted. Indeed, his own desire was that he would be the one worshiped as God.

Eve was deceived, but Adam disobeyed. More importantly, he listened to his wife instead of God. In Genesis 3:17 God says to Adam, "Because you have hearkened to the voice of your wife . . . cursed is the ground for your sake . . ." Adam knew better, yet he chose to honor his wife over God. For this reason he, like both Eve and the serpent, received a curse from God. Adam could have "Just Said No." 1Corinthians 10:13 tells us that "God is faithful, who will not suffer you to be tempted above that you are able; but will with the temptation also make a way to escape, that you may be able to bear it."

Yet, Adam made a willful choice to disobey the command of God.

Why?

I would like to suggest that apart from the literal reading of what actually transpired in the Garden of Eden, something of deeper spiritual significance is occurring here.

Scripture can be studied from a variety of perspectives, including the literal, the metaphorical, the allegorical, the historical, the dispensational, and so on. One way of studying Scripture is to see various types and shadows that are alluded to. Perhaps one of the most well-known types and shadows is that of Melchisedec, who first appears in Genesis 14 and is later discussed in the Book of Hebrews. It is commonly understood that Melchisedec represents and foreshadows Christ. Indeed, Christ is directly associated with him in Hebrews 5:10.

One can also discern principles that are established by accounts of specific events. One such principle is that the elder shall serve the younger. This is found in the account of the births of Esau and Jacob in Genesis 25:23, and perhaps has its fullest expression in the account of Joseph and his brothers.

In the Genesis account of the Fall there is a principle operating, and a type and shadow revealed, which illuminates why Christ's struggle was so intense in the garden of Gethsemane. This is not a new doctrine; rather it is a perspective which may help us understand why so many struggle with their souls even after they have been redeemed from the curse of the law of sin and death.

God is triune—God the Father, God the Son, and God the Holy Spirit. Genesis tells us that God made man in His image, that is, triune. Body, soul, and spirit. The Apostle Paul, in his first letter to the Thessalonians, concludes his writing by saying "I pray God your whole spirit, soul, and body be preserved blameless unto the coming of our Lord Jesus Christ." (1Thessalonianas 5:23) Each of us, then, is a soul created by God, who lives in a body, and has a spirit.

Now, putting these parts together, let's look at the account of the Fall from a fresh perspective, and apply what happened there to what Jesus experiences in the Garden of Gethsemane, and then to our own walk.

Imagine for a moment that as type and shadow Adam represents "spirit" and Eve represents "soul." Of course, each was complete when created in that they both had souls and spirits, as well as individual bodies. I'm simply suggesting a metaphor.

Adam and Eve *together* represent an undivided whole. Spirit and soul in union with God. One plus one equals one. Poor math, perfect theology. Adam in *type* is spirit and Eve in *type* is soul. Soul and spirit, in unity, are one flesh.

The perfection of God.

Spirit is the elder, soul the younger. When Adam hearkens to the voice of his wife he is really hearkening to his the voice of his soul. Mind, will, and emotions rise ascendant over the spirit. Thus, the elder serves the younger. Jesus came, in part, to restore the spirit to its rightful place as master. Nevertheless, the practical application of bringing the soul into submission is no easy task. Paul tells us that this process is one of "working out our salvation with fear and trembling." (Philippians 2:12)

God spoke to Adam, spirit, and gave clear instructions about the trees of the garden. Embrace the Tree of Life, avoid the Tree of the Knowledge of Good and Evil. Presumably, Adam then communicated the admonition of the Lord to Eve. The serpent, or enchanter, appears to Eve, representationally the soul of man, because it is the nature of the soul, or intellect, to reason. Eve, or soul, has a discussion with the serpent and during the dialogue she adds to the Word of God by saying that she has been admonished to not even touch the Tree of the knowledge of good and evil. Clearly, God never said any such thing. Thus, we see the first distortion of God's Word by the reasoning soul and its ultimate consequence.

Have you ever wondered why there were only two trees in the Garden of Eden? Why not three? Logically, it would seem that there should have been the Tree of Life, the Tree of the Knowledge of

18

Good, and then, off by itself—perhaps gnarled and distorted, the ground around it blackened and scorched as a warning—the Tree of the Knowledge of Evil.

But that's not the way it was.

Why?

The Tree of the Knowledge of Good and Evil represents many things to many people. But at its root it ultimately represents magic, enchantment, divination, and witchcraft. 1Samuel 15:23 tells us that "rebellion is as the sin of witchcraft." The rebellion of Adam and Eve in the Garden of Eden, the result of deception and disobedience, is the root of humanity's woes. It is second only to Lucifer's rebellion, the root of all evil. One of the fruits of the Tree of the Knowledge of Good and Evil is magic—both white and black magic. The Good Witch of the North, as well as the Wicked Witch of the East. In reality, there is no such thing as white or black magic. All magic is deception.

Another fruit is humanism. The belief that the thoughts and creations of man are preeminent. The idea that man is basically good, and that through discipline and enlightenment he can achieve equality with God. It is the knowledge of self in opposition to the knowledge of God. The ultimate foolishness—man claiming to be God. Paul tells us in Romans 1:25 that as a result of original Sin, mankind "changed the truth of God into a lie, and worshiped and served the creature more than the Creator." And the prophet Isaiah tells us that it was this desire to be worshiped as God that caused Lucifer to rebel and fall. The famous five "I will's" are set out for us in Isaiah 14:13-14: "I will ascend into Heaven: I will exalt my throne above the stars of God: I will sit also upon the mount of the congregation, in the sides of the north: I will ascend above the heights of the clouds: I will be like the Most High."

If Eve is a type and shadow of the soul, it seems obvious why the serpent appeared to her and deceived her rather than Adam, or spirit. The soul is the seat of the mind, will, and emotions. Satan, in the form of the serpent, appeals to the soul of man, and thus deceives the mind, will, and emotions. James 1:13 tells us that this deception is actually a three step process: (1)"But every man is tempted when he is drawn away of his own lust and enticed (beguiled), (2) Then, when lust has conceived (3) it brings forth sin."

The imagery in the Greek here is very powerful. First, there is deception, an enchantment or beguilement. This implies an active outside force acting on the will. Then, there is a conception, as when a seed is planted in fertile ground and begins to sprout. But this seed must be nourished. If it is not watered and fertilized, it cannot grow. Finally, there is a birth. But what is it that is born?

Sin.

Separation from our Heavenly Father.

In our metaphor, Adam, spirit, the elder, now serves Eve, soul, the younger, as a result of the soul's deception and the spirit's disobedience. Soul and spirit are torn asunder. They are no longer in unity. They are at odds with one another, and with God. With soul ascendant and spirit in submission the stage is set for man's descent into depravity and unrighteousness.

Why is all of this important? Because it lays a foundation for Christ's suffering in the garden of Gethsemane. Hebrews 5:7-10 gives us a powerful picture of Jesus in the garden of Gethsemane:

> **Who in the days of His flesh, when He had offered up prayers and supplications with strong crying and tears unto Him who was able to save Him from death, and was heard in that he feared;**
>
> **Though he were a Son, yet learned He obedience by the things which He suffered;**
>
> **And being made perfect, He became the author of eternal salvation unto all them that obey Him;**
>
> **Called of God a high priest after the order of Melchisedec.**

Three hours. What extraordinary imagery. Christ, God incarnate as man, wrestles with his soul in the garden for three hours. His struggle is so titanic, that He sweats drops of blood. We are told in Hebrews 2:16-18 that Jesus took on the form of man rather than angels because in suffering and overcoming temptation He is able to comfort all of humanity. And Hebrews 4:15 says that Jesus "was in all points tempted like as we are, yet without sin."

Jesus suffered many things during His short time on Earth, including being tempted directly by Satan during his forty days in the wilderness immediately after His baptism by John. Yet, the final battle in Gethsemane was perhaps His greatest test and temptation. Had He not brought His soul into submission in the garden, He would never have gone to the cross. Had Jesus not gone to the cross, everything that He had achieved up to that point would have been extraordinary, but not universally available.

Christ's death and resurrection restored to humanity all that it lost in the Garden of Eden, but it was His victory in Gethsemane that made it possible for all believers to live the victorious life.

What does this mean for us?

It would appear from the condition of the present-day Church that many, perhaps even most, of the Body of Christ have never been to Gethsemane. 1Peter1:9 tells us that "the end of faith is the salvation of your souls." The Greek word translated *"end"* in this passage is *"telos"* and literally means *"completion, or perfection."* Jesus had much to say about the souls of men when He walked among us, not least of which is "he that finds his life (soul) shall lose it: and he that loses his life (soul) for My sake shall find it." (Matthew 10:39) The context of this passage is taking up the cross and following Jesus. In its most basic sense, the idea of taking up the cross means dying to self. It is humbling ourselves before the mighty hand of God and submitting our will to His.

Humility is a fruit of the spirit, i.e., a fruit of the manifest Life of God. Pride is a fruit of the flesh, i.e., a fruit of the manifest life of the soul. The two character traits stand in obvious and direct opposition to one another. The soul's greatest stronghold is pride, and the spirit's greatest weapon is humility. Pride drives a person to rule and reign. Humility draws forth the character of a servant.

Many in the body of Christ today truly desire to take up their cross and follow Jesus, but they just can't seem to stay on it long enough for the nails to be driven in.

A classic example is that of the rich young ruler in Matthew 19. He asks Jesus what he must do to have eternal life. Jesus answers that he is to keep the commandments. The young ruler replies that he has done so from his youth until now and asks what he lacks. Jesus responds, saying, "If you will be perfect, go and sell all you have and give to the poor." This is too much for the man. He left sorrowful because his possessions were of more value to him than what Jesus offered. Although he'd kept all the commandments, and Jesus did not dispute this, the one thing he could not do was give up those things which were the product of, and exalted, his soul.

Many professing Christians today find a similar stumbling block when seeking intimacy with the Lord. The principle elucidated by the story of the rich young ruler is not about having, or not having, possessions. It is about the condition of one's soul. Until an individual learns to *figuratively* take his or her soul to Gethsemane, and thereby put it to death, the message of the Cross will always be simply theology. It will remain impossible for that person to walk in the fullness of what Christ accomplished with the shedding of His precious blood.

The freedom of the Cross cannot, and will not, become reality for us until we allow the Lord to become both the Shepherd *and* the Bishop of our soul. (1Peter 2:25)

It is important to understand that Christ must be *both* our Savior and our Lord for us to walk in the fullness God intends for us. Salvation is the ultimate gift of God, accomplished through the death and resurrection of His precious Son. When we confess Jesus according to Romans 10:9-10 we are saved by the grace of God through faith and His shed blood becomes atonement for our personal sins. It is then that He becomes our personal Shepherd, watching over us as an earthly shepherd watches over and guards his sheep.

Because salvation is a gift, we need only exercise our will and choose to receive the gift by faith. However, we must make another choice as well, and this one is in some respects the more difficult one.

For many, Jesus is their Savior, or Shepherd, but He is not the Lord, or Bishop, of their soul. Bringing the soul into submission is an arduous task for every believer, because the soul has ruled and reigned in our lives since birth. Contrast the picture of the rich young ruler and his possessions with that of Abraham and his son, Isaac. Isaac was Abraham's child of promise, yet, at God's command,

Abraham offered him up as a sacrifice, having the faith that God would honor His word and provide a lamb. Isaac was to Abraham what the rich young ruler's possessions were to him. But Abraham made a very different decision, with very different results. Scripture says that Isaac was Abraham's only son even though Ishmael had been born first. In many ways, Isaac was the fulfillment of the longing in Abraham's soul. However, unlike the rich young ruler, Abraham was willing to give up that which his soul delighted in, and in so doing he reaped eternal reward.

It is the soul in submission that delights God. David sings to the Lord these words in Psalm 131: "Lord, my heart is not haughty, nor mine eyes lofty: neither do I exercise myself in great matters, or in things too high for me. Surely I have behaved and quieted myself as a child that is weaned of his mother: my soul is even as a weaned child." David achieved much in his life, but he also suffered much. Through the things which he suffered he learned to wean his soul from the things of this world.

What is the evidence that we've brought our soul into submission?

The author of Hebrews tells us it is entering into the rest of God and ceasing from our own works. Paul tells us that it is learning to be content in whatever state we are in. James writes that we are to count it all joy when we fall into various temptations because the trying of our faith works patience and when patience is perfected we are then mature, or perfect. And John tells us that the accuser of the brethren, Satan himself, will be cast down and overcome by "the blood of the Lamb" and by those saints who "loved not their lives (souls) unto the death." (Revelation 12:11)

The first Adam's disobedience, because of pride, brought a curse upon mankind—the law of sin and death. The last Adam's obedience, through humility, redeemed us from that curse and made it possible for us to become "partakers of the Divine nature, having escaped the corruption that is in the world through lust." (1 Peter 1:4) However, the willful choice of an individual to accept Christ as Lord and Savior is only the beginning of a process.

The Apostle Paul likens it to the running of a race and tells us that those who run terrestrial races do so in order to obtain a corruptible crown, but those who run the celestial, or spiritual race, do so to receive an incorruptible crown. Writing to the Church at Ephesus he says that the end of this process of salvation is that we will all "come in the unity of the faith, and of the knowledge of the Son of God, unto a perfect man, unto the measure of the stature of the fullness of Christ." (Ephesians 4:13) The Greek word translated *"perfect"* is *"teleios."* A literal translation is *"complete."* The word *"perfect"* here is the same Greek word translated *"end"* in the passage regarding the completion of our faith being the saving of our souls.

Remember the passage in Hebrews 5:9: "and being made *perfect*, He became the author of eternal salvation to all that obey him." That is the same Greek word. *Teleios.* Complete. It is also the same word used in the passage about the rich young ruler, and the passage in James about patience.

Christ came and lived as a man that we might have a living example of how to live a life free from the bondage of sin. He was crucified and shed His precious blood as atonement for that sin. He was resurrected so that all who confess with their mouth that Jesus is Lord, and believe in their heart that God raised Him from the dead might be saved. Once we have accepted Him as Savior, then the process of accepting Him as Lord begins. As we learn to die daily to the demands of our soul, He increases and we decrease. It is then that we will find an increasing intimacy with our Lord.

This principle applies not only to individuals, but to the corporate Body as well. We who comprise the Body of Christ are currently corporately standing in the Garden of Gethsemane. The Church is in a time of crying out to God, "Father if it be Your will, let this cup pass from us." We are now in a season of experiencing Matthew 26 as a corporate Body. There is much agony in the Body as we individually and corporately wrestle with our souls. The soul of the Church is "exceedingly sorrowful, even unto death." There are many in the Body who are like the three who accompanied Christ to the garden, Peter and the two sons of Zebedee. Christ prevailed upon them to "watch and pray," yet each time He returned from His time of travail and prayer He found them asleep. The first time, He admonished Peter, saying, "What, could you not watch with Me one hour?" (Matthew 26:40) Today, Jesus is saying to His Body, "Watch

24

and pray that you do not enter into temptation; the spirit is indeed willing, but the flesh is weak."

We, individually, and more importantly as the corporate Bride of Christ, must say to our Lord and Savior, "O, my Father, if this cup may not pass from us except we drink of it, Your will be done." As we yield to God's desires, laying down our own lives (souls), we please Him. It is not an easy task, but one which God rewards. We may feel at times as if we are "sweating as it were great drops of blood," even as Jesus did. That is why James says, "Count it all joy when you fall into divers temptations; Knowing this, that the trying of your faith works patience, But let patience have her perfect work, that you may be perfect and entire, wanting nothing." (James1:2-4)

There are two different words here for perfect.

The first is the Greek word meaning "*complete in moral character*," while the second means "*whole in body, perfectly sound*." We are complete in Him in both moral character and soundness of body when we allow patience to "have her perfect work" in us. Thus, we see that we become *complete* in Christ when we, like David, wean our souls from the things of this world. This does not mean that we are perfect in the same sense that Christ is perfect because of His deity. Rather, it means that by taking up our cross daily and following after Jesus, we allow "Christ in us, the hope of glory" to bring our souls into submission to His will, His plans, His purposes for us.

Would you like to be perfect, or complete, in Christ?

Then ask yourself this question: Have I ever truly been to Gethsemane?

Two Spirits

—⟊—

In Chapter One we looked at the soul and spirit in light of a biblical type and shadow known as the elder serving the younger, and applied that concept to the process of redeeming, or saving, the soul. In this chapter, I'd like to take the further step of suggesting that there are at least two primary "spirits" that impact the soul. By examining them in light of how they function and interact with one another, we can gain insight to the spiritual battle we all fight on a daily basis.

The two "spirits" I refer to are the political spirit and the religious spirit. Both are birthed in the souls of men, both have their root in the soul's desire for power, both find the source of their strength in legalism, and both have their foundation in rebellion. Each has separate and distinct characteristics, and each seeks to ascend to the pinnacle of authority. Operating individually in the souls of men these "spirits" seek to rule and reign, though by different means. Working in concert, not only do they overthrow nations, they seek to usurp the power of God.

The political spirit arises in the soul of an individual whenever that individual seeks to exalt himself above God. It most often manifests whenever an individual seeks to use intrigue or strategies to obtain a position of power or control. The political spirit takes root in the fallen nature of man, is fertilized by ambition, envy, and jealously, and bears the fruit of rebellion. In its ultimate expression, the political spirit desires to be worshiped as God. Desiring to be "like the Most High God," this spirit drives the individual to change the truth of God into a lie and to worship and serve the creation more than the Creator. In the process, the glory of the incorruptible God is changed into an image made unto the likeness of corruptible man. (Romans 1:25) This is what happened to the children of Israel while Moses was on Mount Sinai, and this is the primary reason they created the golden calf.

The Psalmist tells us that God is King of all the earth (Psalm 47:2), that the Lord is King forever and ever (Psalm 10:16), and that the Lord is the great God and the great King above all gods (Psalm 95:3). There is no other god, or king, before Him. It is He who is the Sovereign power of the universe. Thus, both the political and religious spirit imitate, or emulate, the power of God in a counterfeit fashion.

The political spirit was birthed in the heart of Lucifer when he decided that he would ascend into Heaven, exalt his throne above the stars of God, sit in the mount of the congregation, and be like the Most High God. (Isaiah 14:13-14) It was loosed into the earth when Adam and Eve ate of the Tree of the Knowledge of Good and Evil. The political spirit then grew in the hearts of God's creation until the people determined to make a name for themselves, build a city, and construct a tower that reached into heaven.

Led by Nimrod the people built Babel, Erech, Accad, and Calnah in the land of Shinar. Babylon, the first earthly imperial power, was birthed. The name of this ancient city-state is derived from the Hebrew "*balal,*" meaning to confound, and the Accadian "*babilu,*" meaning gate of God. It was here that God chose to confuse mankind's language and scatter them abroad on the face of the earth to prevent them from continuing in their rebellion.

Nimrod was the sixth son of Cush, Ham's first-born, and it is interesting to note that it was he who rebelled against God. As E.W. Bullinger writes in his work **Number in Scripture**, six is the number of man and often symbolizes man destitute of God or Christ. It can be viewed as the sum of four and two, the creative aspect of God diminished by man's enmity of God, the sum of five and one, God's divine grace made of none effect because of man's perversion or corruption, or the perfection of God, seven, diminished by man's falling short of that perfection.

Nimrod wanted to be worshiped as a king and so he founded his own kingdom. Genesis 10:10 tell us that Nimrod was "a mighty hunter before the Lord." A more literal translation of the Hebrew is that Nimrod was "a mighty hunter who defies the Lord, hunting the souls of men." The text in Genesis suggests that not only did Nimrod want to be *a* king, but that he wanted to be *the* king of the whole Earth. This is one of the main reasons God confounded the language and dispersed the people. It appears that Nimrod's desire to be this type of king mirrored that of Lucifer's. Perhaps that is why Nimrod is often referred to as a type of anti-Christ.

The ultimate act of rebellion in Scripture is that of Lucifer attempting to usurp the power and authority of God. We see this satanic rebellion manifested in Nimrod. The tower built under his direction had at least two purposes. First, it was designed so that at its top was the sanctuary for the god Bel-Merodach, the supreme sun god of the Babylonian pantheon of gods. The second purpose for the tower was to visibly represent in the Earth the unity of all religions under the chief rulership of Bel, or Satan. This was Satan's first attempt to establish a One World religion that worshiped him as God. The tower symbolized the pinnacle of rebellion–false religion and human government working in concert.

Thus, one earthly symbol of the political spirit is a king who usurps the power and authority of God. Two of the best known kings in Scripture are Saul and David. And it is in Saul that we see the fruit of rebellion having significant impact, not only in his own life, but in the lives of the people he ruled.

When God created man, in His own image, He intended that He would forever be the only ruler over His creation. Yet, God's creation was not satisfied with that arrangement. Israel demanded of the prophet Samuel that he "make a king to judge us like all the other nations" and that God was grieved when the people rejected Him as their Sovereign King. (1Samuel 8:6-8) Nevertheless, God warned His people that the kind of king they demanded would be a hard taskmaster and would bring grief and evil to the nation. The people refused to heed the warnings of the prophet appointed by God and insisted that Samuel appoint a king.

Israel's first king is an example to us of how the political spirit operates and manifests in our lives. Whenever we seek to exalt ourselves, instead of allowing God to exalt us, we are manifesting the political spirit. However, when we are humble, God's grace abounds. And when we are patient, and wait upon Him, it is He who exalts us in His time. If we truly desire to see the glory of God manifest in our lives, we must be wary of the traps set by the enemy to lure us into self-exaltation.

Saul's name means *"asked for"* in Hebrew. The Israelites rejected God as their King, cried out in rebellion, and ignored the admonition of the prophet sent by God to set them once again upon the right path. As a result, they got what they asked for. Although Saul seemed to be naturally humble and modest, his strong passions, especially his tendency to be rash in decision making, got him into trouble repeatedly. Ultimately, the fact that he never seemed to be able to accept God unconditionally, nor trust Him implicitly, caused his downfall.

Whenever we place our agenda above God's, we are motivated by pride, and because pride is deceitful we think that we're doing God's will. Often, even though God clearly speaks and commands us, we act out of our own prideful nature. We think we're doing the right thing and yet we have actually sinned against the Lord. Our pride blinds us and causes us to think more highly of ourselves that we ought to. Whenever we presume to walk in a greater authority than we have been given, we tread on very dangerous spiritual ground.

Saul's first transgression against the Lord resulted when he set his will against that of God's and stepped out of the sphere of authority God had granted him as king. Samuel and Saul had agreed to meet at Gilgal in seven days, but Samuel was late. In the meantime, the Philistine army, thirty thousand strong, gathered against Israel. The people grew fearful, while Saul grew impatient. He took on the authority reserved for the priests and sacrificed burnt offerings to the Lord in hopes of gaining God's favor. When Samuel arrived and discovered what Saul had done, he told the king that because of his failure to keep the command of the Lord his kingdom would not continue through his descendants. (1Samuel 13)

What a high price we pay for our disobedience! We would do well to remember that the Lord honors our obedience to Him more than our sacrifices.

Saul never seemed to learn the lesson of obedience. Later, when he was commanded by God, through Samuel, to utterly destroy the Amelikites and all of their possessions and animals, he again disobeyed. Ignoring God's specific and clear command, Saul spared king Agag, along with the best of the sheep, oxen, lambs, and all that was good in the Amelikite camp. This caused God to repent that He had made Saul king. Yet, even when Saul was confronted by Samuel about his transgression, he insisted that he had obeyed the Lord. Samuel replied that Saul's rebellion was the same as witchcraft, and that his stubbornness was the same as idolatry. (1Samuel 15)

Beloved, whenever we presume to believe that we know better than God about a matter, we are partaking of the Tree of the Knowledge of Good and Evil. We saw in Chapter One that the fruit of the Tree of the Knowledge of Good and Evil is magic. A better term is witchcraft.

Witchcraft is counterfeit spiritual authority. Saul was given authority by God to be king. When he forgot the source of his power and acted out of self-will, he stepped out of the realm of his God-given authority. The sin of pride caused him to stumble. When confronted with his sin, instead of repenting, he justified it.

We must remember there is never any justification for sin. There is only atonement. In the Old Testament, that atonement came through blood sacrifice. For believers, the atonement comes through the shed blood of Jesus.

Whenever our own stubborn desires take precedence over obeying the Voice of the Lord, regardless of the immediate outcome of our actions, we ultimately fail. No matter how hard we try to convince others that we have done all which God has commanded us, the fruit of our rebellion will manifest for all to see. Where there is rebellion, there is witchcraft, and where there is stubbornness, or self-will, there is idolatry. Idolatry is worshiping anything other than God as God. If we believe our thoughts are preeminent, we are worshiping our intellect. We are guilty of the same sin as Saul—and

Lucifer. Pride. When pride is allowed to rule in our lives, it ultimately leads us to destruction.

Scripture tells us that God's ways are higher than man's ways, and that His thoughts are higher than our thoughts. God's ways always accomplish His purposes, and His ways will always prosper. (Isaiah 55:9-10) When we hear the Voice of the Lord and we obey, we receive the blessings of God. When we hear and disobey, calamity is our reward. God honors *His* Word, not our *interpretation* of His Word. In essence, He honors Himself. When we align ourselves with His Word, by obeying His commands, we receive a portion of the honor due Him. Not because we are worthy of honor, but because *He* is worthy. Our obedience allows us to partake of the abundant harvest He provides. This is one of the ways we reap the benefit of His sacrifice.

You see, the truest, richest, most costly faith, the faith of great price, comes only through our relationship with a righteous God. We are able to have that relationship only because of the shed blood of His precious Son, Jesus. The Apostle Peter tells us that through the knowledge of God, who has called us to honor and glory, we are given exceedingly great and precious promises and that by these promises we can become partakers of the divine nature and escape the corruption that is in the world through lust. (2Peter1:1-4) The Greek word for knowledge here is *"epignosis"* and means *"full discernment"* or *"to be intimately acquainted with."*

When we are intimately acquainted with the Lord, we partake of *His* Glory and *His* Honor. The Glory and Honor of the Lord is not ours to possess, merely ours to enjoy and benefit from.

I have often heard it said that a man's anointing will make a way for him. While I understand the intent of this statement, I humbly disagree with it. At its root is pride. It is God, and God alone, who removes and sets up kings. Saul is a classic example of a man who believed that his calling as king would make a way for him. A more appropriate statement would be that God raises up whom He will raise up and will open a door that no man can shut. He does this because we keep His Word and do not deny His Name, not because of a perceived anointing. (Revelation 3:8)

Throughout Scripture we see that intimacy with the Lord is characterized by hearing His Voice and obeying. That is our task as believers. We must endeavor to know the Voice of our Lord intimately, and obey quickly, without reservation. Not an easy undertaking, even for the most committed. No wonder we are told that many are called, but few are chosen. In the process, we are likely to stumble, but let it not be because of disobedience, or because of fear of man. Saul repented of his sin, and confessed that he feared the people and obeyed their voice instead of the Voice of God. Nevertheless, even though he repented, was forgiven, and worshiped the Lord, he lost his authority as king—because of pride and rebellion.

If the political spirit is allowed to reign unchecked in our lives, it will ultimately destroy not only our walk with the Lord, but very possibly our life as well. Even though we repent of our sin, often what we have sown still comes to full harvest in our lives.

Whenever we are given opportunities by the Lord to obey His specific command, we must be careful to do so. We must choose the fear of the Lord, over the fear of man, no matter what natural circumstances seem to dictate. We can lose our position of authority, and very possibly our life, when we disobey. Saul lost both. Because of Saul's repeated transgressions, God spoke to Samuel and told him to go to Bethlehem where he would find Israel's next king among the sons of Jesse. Eventually, Saul was mortally wounded on Mount Gilboa, fighting in battle against the Philistines.

If the earthly symbol of the political spirit is the king who usurps God's Kingly authority by embracing and demonstrating a counterfeit authority, then the earthly symbol of the religious spirit is the priest who usurps God's Priestly power by denying it.

Jesus is called our high priest forever, after the order of Melchisedec (Hebrews 6:20), a merciful and faithful priest in things pertaining to God (Hebrews 2:17), and a high priest who is set on the right hand of the throne of Majesty in the heavens. (Hebrews 8:1) When we have intimate relationship with Jesus, we partake of His priestly power, through faith, because of His shed blood. It is our relationship with Him, through His shed blood, that gives us access to the Throne of Grace, and the Father, not simply our confession of faith.

The religious spirit holds to a form of godliness, but denies the power thereof. (2Timothy 3:5) We are admonished by the Apostle Paul to avoid those who have a religious spirit because they have a zeal for God, but no knowledge of Him. (Romans 10:20) Jesus warned that the religious spirit is the "leaven of the Pharisees and Sadducees" (Matthew 16:6) and rebuked those who denied His power saying:

> **"Search the scriptures; for in them you think you have eternal life: and they are they which testify of Me. And you will not come to me that you might have life. I do not receive honor from men. But I know you, that you do not have the love of God in you. I am come in my Father's name, and you receive me not: if another come in his own name, him you will receive. (John 5:39)**

The religious spirit has its foundation in the belief that serving the Lord gains His favor and approval, rather than the acknowledgment that the shed blood of Jesus is the source of our approval. We see this most clearly in Scripture in the context of the Sadducees and Pharisees.

The Sadducees were the aristocrats of Jesus' day, the wealthy and persons of rank. The high priestly families belonged to the Sadducee party. The Sadducees only acknowledged the written Torah, or Law, as binding, and refused to accept the traditions of their fathers as having any legal value. Rigid legalism seems to best sum up their attitude. Additionally, they adamantly rejected the concept of resurrection. In their minds, if Moses, the great lawgiver, did not expressly proclaim it as a doctrine, they were not bound to it as an article of faith.

Yet Jesus, when He was contending with them, rebuked them, saying that they did not know scripture, nor did they know God when He quoted from Moses in Exodus 3:6 saying, "I am the God of Abraham, and the God of Isaac, and the God of Jacob. God is not the God of the dead, but of the living." (Matthew 22:29-33)

The Pharisees, on the other hand, believed in immortality for both the good and the bad. The righteous receive another body, the wicked, eternal torment. The core of their belief was that Fate and God both control man's destiny. The highest calling of man, in their eyes, was to do good works, which God approves of and Fate cooperates in. Ironically, the Pharisees believed that contact with anyone who was unclean, i.e., all non-Jews or heathens, produced defilement, and so they avoided such individuals religiously, even Jews who were not Pharisees.

This is why the Pharisees found fault with Jesus when He spent time with publicans and sinners. (Mark 2:14-17) Piety was the Pharisees chief goal. To that end, they took great pains to elevate form over substance, outward observances over inward regeneration, and petty details over the great truths of life. The Pharisees fervently sought the admiration of men, engaged in vain and trifling questions, and consistently sought to entrap the unwary with cunning arguments. They sought not to glorify God, but rather their own narrow views. They prided themselves on the exclusive nature of their sect, and worked fervently to gain converts.

When legalism and zealousness come together in the soul, they produce a mindset that rejects the power of God and attributes it to works of the flesh, or worse, the devil. Jesus was accused of casting out demons by the power of Beelzebub, the ruler of demons. But He admonished the scribes who accused Him to be careful in what they said, lest they be guilty of blaspheming the Holy Spirit. It is one thing to accuse the Son of operating in witchcraft, quite another to attribute the work of the Holy Spirit to the devil. The former is forgivable, the latter, a sin which results in eternal damnation. (Mark 3:23-30)

The driving force behind the religious spirit is fear.

We must be very careful not to allow fear, especially of the unknown, to cause us to stumble. We must also guard against thinking that we can know God through the power of intellect. The Apostle Paul warned the Corinthian church about this attitude when he said, "The natural man receives not the things of the Spirit of God, for they are foolishness unto him; neither can he know them because they are spiritually discerned." (1Corinthians 2:14) Knowing *about* God and *knowing Him intimately* are two different things.

Watchman Nee, in his work **The Ministry of God's Word**, makes the point that because God is light, His thoughts are light. When our minds receive a revelation of the Word of God, it comes to us in the form of light. Light, by its nature, is not containable. When the Light of God illumines us, we must somehow capture it and hold on to it so that we can understand it and benefit from it. Nee points out that, if we have a thought life that has been disciplined to focus on the Lord, instead of the things of this world, we are able to apprehend the revelation, hold on to it, and translate it into a usable format. This is how we are transformed—by the renewing of our mind. The power of intellect pales when compared with the power of the Holy Spirit. It is not by might, nor by power, but by the spirit of the living God that we overcome.

Knowing *about* God, bereft of a true relationship with Him, breeds a legalistic self-righteousness. Pride sustains it, and fear fuels it. True intimacy, on the other hand, is born of familiarity, and familiarity requires spending time in His presence. When we spend time in His presence we receive revelation, not only *of* His Word, but of *The Word* made flesh. And this causes us to want to crucify our flesh, so that our spirit might rise preeminent.

When He increases, we decrease.

One who has an intimate revelation of Jesus as both Savior and Lord knows that true righteousness can only come from the One who is truly righteous, through the grace of God, and not because of any legal basis. As we saw earlier, righteousness is not something one has or possesses; rather, it is something one *partakes of*, because the soul is in submission to the spirit, the result of an intimate relationship with Jesus. This is why Paul writes to the Galatians:

> **"I have been crucified with Christ; it is no longer I who live, but Christ lives in me; and the life which I now live in the flesh I live by faith in the Son of God, who loved me and gave Himself for me.**
> **I do not set aside the grace of God; for if righteousness comes through the law, then Christ died in vain."**
> **(Galatians 2:20-21)**

If we judge and condemn the unfamiliar out of fear, we risk missing what God is saying or doing. When Moses led Israel out of Egypt, at the command of God, and Pharaoh pursued them to the shores of the Red Sea, the people grew fearful and rebelled against Moses. They accused God's appointed leader of delivering them from Egypt, only to let them die in the wilderness. Moses replied, "Do not be afraid. Stand still and see the salvation of the Lord, which He will accomplish for you today . . . The Lord will fight for you and you shall hold your peace." (Exodus 14:13-14)

When we allow our intellect and reason to override what God has spoken into our lives through His Word, we risk losing much. However, if we cultivate our thought life so that it is focused on those things which are spiritually discerned, and we endeavor to hear His Voice on a daily basis, then we will see His majesty and splendor manifest in ways which will astound us and glorify Him.

If fear is the driving force of the religious spirit, then pride—in the form of idealism—is the vehicle which fear fuels. Idealism seeks to preserve God's glory by demanding high standards of accountability. While it is important to be accountable, God needs no man, nor any set of standards or laws, to preserve His Glory. Fear and pride go hand in hand, and they are a deadly duo for those who would seek intimacy with the Father. It is one thing to be ignorant of the ways of the Lord and to be genuinely cautious about claims of supernatural power. But we must not allow our caution to turn into prejudice, resentment, or hatred, through pride in our high standards.

The religious spirit seeks perfection above all else—perfection in doctrine, lifestyle, even in relationship with Jesus. The religious spirit is the spirit of anti-Christ, or, perhaps more accurately, the spirit of "instead-of-Christ." The soul in which the religious spirit is strong seeks to gain attention for itself. Most often, it does this by demanding recognition in the form of a title, or a claim, to a position. Contrast this spirit, with the Spirit in Jesus, a man who was a carpenter and sought no other man's recognition.

If we desire intimacy with the Father, through the Son, we must put aside our soul's desire to be recognized and exalted. We must lay down any claim to fame we think we have and seek to serve, rather than be served. It is in this process of breaking the outward man that the inward man comes into an intimate relationship with the Lord. Often, God allows circumstances in our life to accomplish this purpose. How well we respond to those circumstances determines the degree to which our soul is in submission to the Holy Spirit, and the degree to which God can use us for His ultimate purposes.

We have looked at both the political spirit and the religious spirit in light of their characteristics, and their manifestation. Both originate in the soul, germinate with the application of fear and pride, and then grow to full stature under the intellect's guiding hand. Each can operate independently of the other, with profound affect; but it is when these two spirits come together in unity that they are the most powerful, and the most dangerous, to the life of the soul.

The political spirit tried to kill Jesus when He was yet an infant. Herod the Great ordered that all children under the age of two be slaughtered, because he had heard that the "King of the Jews" had been born. He was fearful his power would be usurped. The religious spirit tried to take Christ's life by stoning Him, when He claimed to be one with God. But it took both the political and religious spirit, working together, to crucify the Lord of Glory. And then, only because He willed it to be so.

These two spirits operate the same way in our souls.

The political spirit operates to kill Christ in us by manipulating us to seek power and authority that are not rightfully ours. It drives us to use cunning and manipulation to achieve our goals, rather than having the faith to wait upon the Lord to establish us in our rightful authority. The soul which is not in submission to the spirit seeks to kill anything which it thinks will prevent it from gaining recognition, rather than killing that thing in it which desires recognition. When we begin to think higher of ourselves than we ought to, we are engaging in idol worship.

Many today hold to a so-called "New Age" philosophy that every human being has "god potential" within them. Sin becomes nothing more than "negative thinking" which must be purged and replaced with "positive thinking." Morality for the New Age thinker no longer finds its genesis in absolutes, but rather in relativistic thinking. Christ, the Son of God who died to take away the sins of the world, becomes "the Christ-spirit" within us. His exalted position as Immanuel, God with us, God in us, is reduced to a mere shadow of deity, that of a "highly evolved member of our species," or simply "the spirit of good in all of us."

In New Age philosophy, the soul is elevated to a position of preeminence. Reincarnation is used to explain how, and why, the soul regenerates in physical form. The biblical reality, "it is appointed unto man once to die, then the judgment" (Hebrews 9:27) is ignored, or worse, denigrated as a narrow-minded religious doctrine which impedes the evolution of mankind into a higher consciousness. If we are all "gods" New Age philosophy tells us, then we have the power to create our own reality, whether good or bad. Everything that happens to us is simply a mirror of our thought life. We control our destiny, we control how many times our soul is regenerated in physical form so that we can "get it right." We control the speed at which we "evolve" into a being that is truly godlike. Sound familiar? Remember Lucifer's five "I wills," the last of which was "I will be like the Most High."

The religious spirit seeks to kill Christ in us by distorting the true priestly ministry. This spirit gains power in our souls as it places undue influence upon sacrifice, perverting the admonition for us to take up our crosses daily. Thus, the religious spirit is founded in a works mentality. This attitude stands in opposition to Scripture, which tells us we are saved by "grace through faith . . . not of works lest any man should boast." (Ephesians 2:8-9)

The religious spirit also causes us to mistrust anything we don't understand, and can't control.

Jezebel is an example in the Old Testament, while King Herod's wife is an example in the New. Confounded by the ministry of Elijah, Jezebel, the wife of King Ahab, sought to have him destroyed. However, it was she who was destroyed and Elijah who prevailed. Elijah's ministry was that of preparing the way of the Lord, as was John the Baptist's. When John the Baptist spoke out against Herod's adultery with his brother Phillip's wife, Herod put him in prison and later beheaded him because of his wife's manipulations.

In Revelation 2:20-24 the church at Thyatira was rebuked because they had allowed "that woman Jezebel, who calls herself a prophetess, to teach and seduce." As a result of her false teachings, the servants of the Lord were committing sexual immorality and eating things sacrificed to idols. The Lord was patient, and gave her time to repent, but said He would cast those who "commit adultery with her into great tribulation." Jezebel appears to have been a prominent woman in the city of Thyatira, a city famous for its magnificent temple of Diana, the Greek goddess of the moon. In 1Kings16 we read that king Ahab's wife, Jezebel, introduced the worship of Astarte, the Canaanite goddess associated with fertility, into Israel, and here in the Book of Revelation we see another woman named Jezebel promoting the worship of Diana. Yet the First Commandment says, "you shall have no other gods before me." (Deuteronomy 5:7)

Our faith must always be in the sacrifice Jesus made, never in our own sacrifices. We will never manipulate God to move on our behalf by working harder, or making sacrifices to Him. We cannot purchase His Grace, or His Glory. When we try to crucify our flesh, the result is *self*-righteousness. When the Lord crushes us, He does so with a firm, but gentle hand, with the intent of bringing forth the sweet smelling savor of the fruit within us. "For whom the Lord loves, He chastens, and scourges every son whom He receives." (Hebrews 12:6)

This is the true message of Gethsemane.

We spoke earlier of two of the most notable kings in the Bible — Saul and David. If Saul is to be an example to us of what not to do, then David is our example of a man after God's own heart. Apart from Jesus, Moses and David are the two men in Scripture in whom we see the manifestation of both the kingly and priestly functions in proper perspective. Although Moses spoke with God face-to-face, it is in David that we see the clearest scriptural example of the kind of heart in a man that God finds pleasing.

This does not mean that David was perfect.

Far from it.

David was a man of war. Because of this, the Lord did not allow him to fulfill his desire to build God an earthly house. Yet, because of his faithfulness, his son Solomon was given that right. David committed adultery, and murder. Yet, he is mentioned as a hero of faith in Hebrews 11. Why? Because the Lord knows our hearts better than we ever will. When He was instructing Samuel about the sons of Jesse, He said, "Do not look at physical appearance or stature, because I have refused him. For the Lord does not see as a man sees; for man looks at the outward appearance, but the Lord looks at the heart." (1Samuel 16:7)

Kevin J. Connor, in his work **The Tabernacle of David,** points out that David is the only man in Scripture who received three distinct anointings, and these anointings foreshadow our Lord.

David was anointed first as a prophet. The prophetic anointing is representative of the Ministry of the Word of God. With the eyes of a seer, David saw, and wrote about, the sufferings of Jesus, and the Glory that would result from His obedience. This first anointing was both literal and figurative. Samuel took a horn of oil and literally poured the holy anointing oil over David at the command of the Lord.

David's second anointing, as king over the house of Judah, signified the Ministry of Reigning and Ruling. The kingly anointing. This was David's dominant office and foreshadows Jesus as our King. One obvious attribute of the kingly anointing is power over the enemy. Although persecuted and hated by his enemies, David ultimately prevailed. Likewise, Jesus, despised of men, overcame the ultimate enemy, death, and by His resurrection made it possible for us to partake of God's eternal Life.

When David was anointed as a shepherd boy, called out by Samuel from among his seven brothers, he was being anointed to become king *in God's appointed time.* David was tested by the Word of God, as his ancestor Joseph had been, then he was anointed king over Judah, or praise, where he reigned seven and one half years.

David's final anointing was the priestly anointing, which signifies the Ministry of Reconciliation. This priestly anointing foreshadows the high priest anointing of the order of Melchisedec, which is the King-Priest. The priestly anointing combines intercession, prayer, worship, and praise unto God. David received this anointing only after he was made king over all Israel. Israel literally means, *"having power with God"* or *"God's fighter."* David was thirty years old when he was made king over all Israel, the same age Christ was when He began His ministry, and he reigned over all Israel for thirty-three years, the same age Jesus was when He was crucified.

Moses, David, and Jesus are the three men in Scripture who successfully combined the offices of Prophet, Priest, and King into one person. Each built a tabernacle, but only Jesus built the "greater and more perfect tabernacle, not made with hands." (Hebrews 9:11) Immediately after David was anointed king at Hebron, he captured Zion, the City of David. Jerusalem—City of Peace. It was then and there that he set up the Tabernacle of David which symbolized both the Davidic Kingdom, in the form of David's lineage and throne, and the Davidic Worship, in the form of the Ark of the Covenant. David's kingly heritage represents the results of God-given authority to rule and reign, while his priestly heritage represents the result of true worship.

When God-inspired authority and God-inspired worship unite in our souls, the true kingly and priestly anointings are made manifest in the form of *The* King and *The* Priest, Jesus.

It is then that His Glory is revealed in us and through us.

It is then that we are transformed.

The Greek word for transformed is *metamorphoo* and it is used in only four passages of Scripture. The first and second uses are in Matthew 17:2 and Mark 9:2, where each refers to the "transfiguration" of Christ in the presence of Peter, James, and John. God announces to the apostles that this is His beloved Son "in whom He is well pleased," and commands them to listen to what He has to say. The third usage is in Romans 12:2 and refers to the transformation of the believer by the "renewing of the mind." The Apostle Paul admonishes us not to "be conformed to the world" while simultaneously informing us that the renewing, or transforming, of our mind will allow us to manifest what is agreeable, well-pleasing, and complete in the sight of God.

But it is in the fourth and final passage that all of the key elements come together. When we listen to what Jesus has to say, and allow Him, through the power of the Holy Spirit, to transform our minds, it is then that we both understand, and partake, of the ultimate intent of the Father:

But we all, with open face, beholding as in a glass the Glory of the Lord, are *changed (transformed) into the*

same image **from glory to glory, as by the Spirit of the Lord. (2Corinthians 3:18) (Italics mine)**

On the other hand, when the political or religious spirit rises in us, and our souls yield to either one—or both—of them, calamity awaits us. King Saul and King Uzziah are scriptural examples of men who exceeded the kingly and priestly authority given them by God. Both of them paid dearly for their presumptive behavior. Saul, as we have seen, grew impatient. He offered sacrifices unto the Lord, instead of waiting for Samuel the Prophet-Priest to do it. King Uzziah usurped the authority of the priests by burning incense, and was smitten by God with leprosy.

We must be careful not to exceed the authority given to us by God, lest we reap the reward of our presumptive behavior. We must also be aware of the battle in, and for, our soul. Both the political spirit and the religious spirit desire to "make the word of God of none effect" in our lives through our secular and religious traditions. (Mark 7:13) If we truly desire to see the Glory of God manifest in our lives, it is not enough to simply "fight the good fight of faith." We must also use the measure of faith given to us by God to reign in, and take authority over, those areas in our soul where we consistently give place to the enemy of our soul. If we purpose in our hearts that He must increase, we *will* decrease.

This is why Jesus went to Gethsemane.

This is why He took three hours, as a man, to wrestle with His soul.

The cross was a torturous necessity, because there is "no remission of sin without the shedding of blood." (Hebrews 9:22) It was Christ's death and resurrection that freed us from being slaves to sin. But it was the battle He won at Gethsemane which assured you and me, as Believers, that the Lord will redeem the soul of His servants, and that none who trust in Him will be desolate. (Psalm 34:22)

Hebron

—∿∿—

Today, Hebron is one of the most volatile cities in Israel, primarily because all three major religions—Judaism, Christianity, and Islam—consider it a holy site. The most famous historical site in the city is the Cave of the Machpelah, the Cave of the Prophets. According to Jewish tradition, Abraham, Sarah, Isaac, Rebekah, Jacob, and Leah are all buried here. Because of this, throughout history, churches, synagogues, and mosques have been built on the site.

But there is something even more significant about Hebron.

Spiritually, Hebron represents the place of *covenant union* with God. It is located in the mountains of Judah, almost equidistant from Beersheba and Jerusalem, just over three thousand feet above the Mediterranean. It is the highest city in Israel. Its name is derived from the Assyrian word which means *"to be joined,"* or *"to bind."*

Hebron is first mentioned in Genesis, in connection with Abram. The Lord spoke to Abram, while he was living in Haran. He instructed the patriarch to leave his country, his family, and his father's house. The Lord promised Abram that He would make of him a great nation, bless him, make his name great, and make him a blessing to others. The Lord further promised He would bless those who blessed Abram, curse those who cursed him, and that through him all the families of the earth would be blessed. (Genesis 12:1-3)

Abram's first stop on his journey to Canaan was the plain of Moreh, not far from Shechem. Moreh, in Hebrew, means" *instruction"* or *"teaching."* It was here, at Moreh, that the Lord appeared

45

to Abram and said, "Unto your seed will I give this land." (Genesis 12:7)

It is worthwhile to point out a significant progression.

First, the Lord speaks, giving a command coupled with the promise of a blessing. "Leave behind all that you know, all familiarity, obey My command, and not only will I bless you, but I will make you a blessing to others." Abram was asked to give up much, but he was also promised much. The key to receiving the promised blessing of God for Abram was not sacrifice, but obedience.

So it is for us.

Next, once Abram heard and obeyed, the Lord appeared to him at the place of instruction or teaching and gave him a specific, non-conditional promise: "Unto your seed will I give this land." At that point, the blessing was now officially Abram's to possess. God's Word went forth, and did not return unto Him void, because, as the prophet Jeremiah tells us, God watches over His Word to perform, or hasten, it. (Jeremiah 1:12)

Because of God's great love, He chooses to bless us. The Apostle John records the following words of Jesus: "He that has My commands and keeps them, he it is that loves Me: and he that loves Me shall be loved of My Father, and I will love him, and will manifest Myself to him." (John 14:21) The Greek word for manifest means to "openly exhibit or appear." This is a very exciting promise for anyone who desires a more intimate relationship with the Lord.

When the Lord reveals Himself to us *openly* in the place of instruction or teaching we are forever changed. It is then a burning desire rises within us and draws us closer and closer to Him.

As a result of the Lord's appearance, and His promise, Abram built an altar on the spot and gave thanks to the Lord. Then, immediately after that awesome physical encounter with the Lord, he pitched his tent between *Beit-El*, "House of God" and *Ai*, "the Ruin," built a second altar, and called upon the name of the Lord.

Let's look at what this represents for us.

Ai represents the consequences of disobedience to the Lord. It was at *Ai* that Israel was defeated in battle, because of the sin of Achan in disobeying the command of the Lord, after the destruction of Jericho. Achan means *troublesome* in Hebrew. When Achan's sin was discovered, he and his family were stoned, and the site became known as the Valley of Achor, or the Valley of Trouble. When we ignore the command of the Lord, and are disobedient, we open the door for trouble and calamity, not only for ourselves, but for our family as well.

Beth-el, on the other hand, represents the place where we have intimate fellowship with the Lord. It is the site where Jacob had his dream of angels ascending and descending to heaven, where God reiterated the promise he gave to Jacob's grandfather, Abram. Here, also, the Lord promised Jacob He would not leave him until He accomplished that which He had promised. (Genesis 28:12-19) The original Canaanite name for *Beth-el* is Luz, *the almond tree.* In Hebrew, the word for almond is *"shaqed,"* which means *"the awakening one."* It is the first of the fruit trees to blossom, usually in late January or early February. Interestingly, there is an allusion to another of the meanings of the Hebrew root, which can mean *"to hasten,"* as we saw above in Jeremiah 1:11-12.

When we meet with God, in the house of God, we "awaken" and He "hastens" to perform His Word.

What marvelous imagery!

Up to this point, God is the pursuer, and Abram the pursued. But then, once Abram not only hears the Lord's Voice, but *sees* Him as well, something exciting happens.

Abram begins to pursue the Lord.

An interesting parallel can be drawn between Abram's experience and that of Moses. Moses hears the Voice of the Lord calling out to him from within the burning bush. He obeys the Lord's command by returning to Egypt and confronting Pharaoh. Then, he asks to see the glory of the Lord on Mount Sinai. God honors his request, as we will see in Chapter Seven

In both of these examples, we see an important principle demonstrated—God speaks, man hears and obeys, God manifests.

What does this mean for us?

The key for those who desire to see the glory of God *visibly demonstrated* in their lives on a daily basis, is to earnestly seek to hear His Voice, and then obey His commands. Jesus assures us that if we are His sheep, we hear His Voice, we follow Him, and that no man can pluck us out of His hand. (John 10:27-28) We are also told that obedience is better than sacrifice. (1Samuel 15:22). The Lord does not desire our sacrifices. He desires that we incline our ear to hear His voice, and then obey His commands to the best of our ability. The ultimate sacrifice has already been offered–Jesus. It remains only for us to seek an intimate relationship with the Son, so that we might please the Father. Jesus came and walked as a man, then died and was resurrected, so that the wall of partition between God and his creation could be forever torn asunder.

In Hebron, the Lord expands upon, and confirms, His earlier promise to Abram.

Abram's nephew, Lot, traveled with his uncle to Canaan. Disagreement arose between the herdsmen of Lot's cattle and Abram's herdsman. With great wisdom, and magnanimity, Abram gives Lot first choice of the land that God had promised to give to him. Lot chooses the plains of Jordan, Abram takes the hill country. Later, God instructs Abram to look out as far as he can see from his lofty position — to the north, south, east, and west — saying all the land he sees will be given to him and his descendants forever. The Lord goes on to promise that Abram's descendants will be as numerous as the specks of dust on the earth. The Abrahamic Covenant is established, and it will have profound implications for the entire future history of mankind.

Once again, as a result of his encounter with God, Abram builds an altar — this time in Hebron.

If we desire to enter into *covenant union* with God, we must go *spiritually* to Hebron. This does not mean the believer lacks a covenant *relationship* with the Lord; it means that in order to have a deeper, more intimate relationship with our Lord and Savior, we must go to the place where we can clearly hear His Voice, we must abide there, and then we must obey His instruction. When we hear and obey, He openly manifests Himself to us. It is then that the desire to build an altar in our heart, and give thanks unto Him, rises within us.

In the case of the believer, the location of the altar is in our heart.

As Paul tells us, we are the temple of the Living God. He dwells in us, and walks with us. He is our God, and we are His people.

(2Corinthians 6:16) Who shall ascend into the hill of the Lord? Who shall stand in His holy place? He that has clean hands and a pure heart; who has not lifted up his soul to vanity, nor sworn deceitfully. (Psalm 24:3-4)

A common saying in Israel is that one always goes "up to Jerusalem," never "down." When we accept Christ as our Savior, in a sense, we "go up" from eternal death to life everlasting. Salvation is the first, yet most crucial, step in our relationship with God. Romans 10:9-10 tells us that we must first believe in our heart, then confess with our mouth, that Jesus is who He claimed to be. It is only because of Jesus the Son that we can even think of having an intimate relationship with God the Father. Jerusalem means the *"place of peace."* Jesus is called, among other names, the Prince of Peace, because it is He who brings lasting peace into our hearts. It is He who turns hearts of stone into hearts of flesh. In so doing, Jesus, the Light of the world, is the Light Who illuminates the Father. Everything Jesus did on this earth, as a man, was intended to reflect and reveal God the Father.

Paul tells the men of Athens that it is in Jesus that "we live, and move, and have our being." (Acts 17:28) It is Jesus who knew us from the foundations of the world. It is Jesus who seeks us out, calling us by name. It is Jesus who numbers the hairs on our heads. It is in Jesus, and in Him alone, that we move from death unto life.

From salvation to intimacy. From glory to glory. Line upon line, precept upon precept, Jesus is always wooing and seducing us into a deeper intimacy with Him.

The Psalmist tells us that deep calls unto deep.

We begin our salvation experience believing, as did the Shulamite woman, "my beloved is mine and I am His." But, as Jesus reveals Himself more fully, as we are drawn into an ever-deeper, ever-more intimate relationship with Him, as He increases and we decrease, we end up knowing, as she did, that "I am my beloved's and His desire is toward me." (Song of Solomon 2:16, 7:10)

Hebron is higher than Jerusalem physically by several hundred feet. Similarly, the place of covenant union with our Lord is a higher place in the spirit than the place of peace wrought in our heart by virtue of our salvation and our blossoming relationship with the

Lord. It is a difficult climb in the natural to Hebron from Jerusalem. Likewise, it is a difficult ascent in the spirit to enter the place of intimacy with our Lord.

In the life of David we see a representation of a man who was on intimate terms with the Lord. A man, Scripture tells us, after God's own heart. David was wrongly accused and pursued by Saul, yet he refused to touch the Lord's anointed king. After Saul's death, David lamented, then inquired of the Lord, saying, "Shall I go up into any of the cities of Judah?" (2Samuel 2:1) In Hebrew, Judah means *"God be praised."* God answers David and tells him to go "up" to Hebron.

The place of *"community."* The place *"to be joined."* The place of *"binding."*

David took his two wives with him—Ahinoam the Jezreelitess, and Abigail, the Carmelite.

Ahinoam means *"grace,"* and Jezreel means *"God sows."* Abigail, David's favorite wife, means *"joy."* She was from Carmel, which when rendered in the Hebrew as a common noun means a *"fruitful or plentiful field."*

If we desire intimacy with our Lord, we must first enter into His praise. We must "go up" spiritually to the cities of Judah—specifically, to Hebron—to the place where we are "joined" with Him. The two attitudes we must carry with us in the spirit, are the *grace* He has sown into our hearts, and the *joy* which gushes forth from a fruitful heart.

David carried five stones with him when he confronted Goliath. Some scholars suggest that Goliath had four brothers. Perhaps he did. However, five is the number of grace. David's faith was in God, not in his own strength. It was by God's grace that he slew the giant who had intimidated all of Saul's army. So too, by the grace of God, the giants in our lives can be slain. Then, like David, we can take the heads of our Goliaths up to Jerusalem, to the place of peace, where we will be met by the Great King.

The Psalmist tells us that God will show us the path of life. In His presence is fullness of joy, and at His right hand are pleasures forevermore. (Psalm 16:11) Joy opens the gates of our heart to receive all the Lord has for us. We must go up to Hebron in the spirit, rejoicing in our heart, believing that the statutes of the Lord are right, believing His commandments are pure, enlightening our eyes, and believing that His judgments are true and righteous.

Our God never changes. He is the same yesterday, today, and forever. No matter what we encounter in this life, God is there ahead of us. We must grasp hold of this important truth, as David did: "The trial of our faith being much more precious than of gold that perishes, though it be tried with fire, might be found unto praise and honor and glory at the appearing of Jesus Christ: whom having not seen, you love: in whom, though now you see Him not, yet believing, you rejoice with joy unspeakable and full of glory." (1Peter 1:7-9)

What did David do when he arrived in Hebron?

"And his men that were with him did David bring up, every man with his household: and they *dwelt* in the cities of Hebron. (2Samuel 2:3) God wants us to *dwell* with Him in the place of binding—in the place of intimacy. We are called to *abide* there and maintain worship and praise. Some have said that intimacy really means "Into-Me-See." This was the desire of Moses when he asked the Lord to see His glory. He had already heard the Voice of the Lord, and spoken with the Him face-to-face, but he wanted more. He wanted to behold God's Glory, and he was persistent. So persistent, that God finally relented.

When we behold the Glory of God, we cannot help but be changed. When we spend time in God's presence, and His Glory bathes us, we are never the same. When we abide with the King of the Universe, we cannot help but be transformed. Scripture tells us that when Moses came down from the mountain of God, after being in the presence of the glory of God for forty days and nights, the skin of his face shined with such glory that Aaron and the people were afraid to come near him. (Exodus 34:29-30)

What a wonderful thing it would be if we engendered such fear in those around us.

Jesus tells us that if we abide in Him, and He abides in us, we will bear much fruit. Dwelling in the place of covenant union with God, abiding in the place of intimacy, praising Him in the place of binding, causes us to bear fruit. The Psalmist tells us that the man who does not walk in the counsel of the ungodly, who does not stand in the way of sinners, who does not sit in the seat of the scornful, that man will take delight in the law of the Lord. He will meditate on God's law both day and night. As a result, he "shall be like a tree planted by the rivers of water, that brings forth his fruit in his season; his leaf also shall not wither and whatsoever he does shall prosper." (Psalm 1:1-3)

David was very fruitful in Hebron.

His wives bore him six sons—Amnon, Chileab, Absalom, Adonijah, Shephatiah, and Ithream.

Amnon, meaning *"faithful,"* was his first-born. The first-born in Jewish tradition is the priest of the family. Jesus, the first-born of many, is our High Priest, after the order of Melchisedec. He is called Faithful and True. (Revelation 19:11) Our God is a faithful God, and He keeps covenant to a thousand generations. He will not allow us to be tempted above what we are able to resist. In every temptation He provides us a way out. In the place of joining, in the place of intimacy, in the place of binding, as we dwell in His presence, we become faithful to His Word. Like Moses, we then have the opportunity to become faithful in all things.

Chileab, the *"perfection of the Father,"* was born of Abigail, *"joy."* As we delight in the Lord, and take joy in His Presence, we experience His perfect love. Our fears begin to dissolve. We leave behind doubt and uncertainty. In His presence is joy forevermore. The joy of the Lord becomes our strength. We rise above circumstances, as the Apostle Paul did, and praise Him in the midst of our pain and suffering.

Absalom, *"Father of Peace,"* was David's third son. In the place of intimacy, there is peace. Jesus is called the Prince of Peace, and it is He who sets us free from worry and concern. We are told that if we love the law of God, we will have great peace, and nothing shall offend us. (Psalm 119:165) Imagine the freedom. Imagine the power of being dead to every offense.

Adonijah, *"YHWH is Lord,"* was David's fourth son. Jesus is Lord of all. His is the Name above all names. "By Him were all things created, that are in heaven and earth, visible and invisible . . . all things were created by Him and for Him." (Colossians 1:16) In the place of binding, Jesus becomes not only our Savior, but our

Lord. As we experience His awesome Sovereignty in our lives, we, like Paul, begin to see ourselves as His bond slave. We come to understand that our life is not our own, because we were bought with His precious blood. It is then that we are able to take up our cross and die daily to our selfish desires. It is then that we mortify our flesh, and bring our soul into submission, even as David did.

Shephatiah, *"God has judged,"* was David's fifth son. Five is the number of grace. In Hebron, we are judged as we bake in the white-hot fire of intimacy. Yet, God's judgment is tempered with His grace. It is His grace that saved us, and it is His grace that sustains us during our time of judgment. We must leave behind all pretense, all pride. Whatever is not of God will be consumed, leaving only the pure gold of our faith. We are admonished to "come boldly to the throne of grace, that we may obtain mercy, and find grace to help in time of need." (Hebrews 4:16) God's merciful and righteous judgment transforms us. We must understand and embrace the fact that He scourges those whom He loves.

We are pruned that we might bring forth fruit. As we endure, as Job did, we grow—from children, to young men, to fathers. As children, we simply know *about* Him. Many know the Book of the Lord, but few know the Lord of the Book. As young men, the Word of God grows strong in us. Through faith we overcome the wicked one, the accuser of the brethren. As fathers, we intimately know Him who was from the beginning. He becomes not only our Great Shepherd, but the Lord of our life. He no longer calls us servants, but friends.

Ithream was the sixth son of David born in Hebron. His name means *"remnant or abundance of the people."* Five is the number of grace, and seven the number of spiritual perfection. Six represents the number of man. Hence, while we walk this Earth, we are forever moving between grace and perfection, seeking to become more than we are, yet knowing we are merely a shadow of what we become when we take on His likeness. His grace sustains and uplifts us through the process of spiritual growth. His perfect love ever draws us to Him.

In Hebron, Grace and Love collide.

By His grace, and through His love, we become fitly joined to the body of Christ. No longer Lone Rangers, we come into unity with others who seek His glory. As we abide in Him, and dwell in His presence, and praise Him together in unity, we experience His abundance in all things. We learn, as did Paul, to be content in whatever condition we are in. (Philippians 4:11)

In Hebron, we experience His faithfulness, His perfection, His peace, His sovereignty, His judgment, and His abundance. We discover God is more interested in relationship than religion, that He is more interested in the condition of our heart, than in the magnitude of our works. As we dwell with Him in the place of intimacy, the place of binding, and behold His glory, we are transformed into the likeness of His image.

He increases, and we decrease.

We become consumed with an overwhelming desire to set up our tents in His presence and live there forever, as were Peter, James, and John on the Mountain of Transfiguration.

A well-known song says, "Cast your eyes upon Jesus, look full into His wonderful face, and the things of this world become strangely dim, in the light of His glory and grace." Oh, that it could be said of us all, as it was said of Peter and John, that we are ignorant and unlearned people, but that we have been with Jesus. (Acts 4:13)

When we abide with the Father in Hebron, the place of intimacy, we also receive the blessing of His anointing. "And the men of Judah came, and there they anointed David king over the house of Judah. (2Samuel 2:4) It is fitting that in Hebron David was first anointed king over "*the house of praise*," then anointed king over Israel, "*power with God.*" Once we understand that praise unlocks the power of intimacy with God, we begin to walk in a dimension of authority many desire, but few ever attain. David spent seven and one half years ruling from Hebron, then thirty-three years ruling from Jerusalem. When we are faithful with little, we are given much. When we are faithful in praise and worship, we walk in power. We then rule from the place of peace. When we humble ourselves under the mighty hand of God, He exalts us in due time. (1Peter 5:6)

In Ugaritic, Hebron means "*community.*" In Hebron, the place of community, we find our place in God's kingdom. In Hebron, the place of joining, prophetic promises are activated. In Hebron, the place of binding, we enter into covenant relationship with our Lord. In Hebron, we grow strong while our enemies grow weak. "Now there was a long war between the house of Saul and the house of David: but David waxed stronger and stronger, and the house of Saul waxed weaker and weaker." (2Samuel 3:1)

In the place of binding, in the place of intimacy, in the place of community, we learn, as Joshua did, that the battle is truly the Lord's. As the walls of Jericho were brought down with a unified shout, so shall all the Jerichos in our own lives be brought down to rubble when we lay hold to the truth spoken by Isaiah ". . . who will contend with me? . . . who is my adversary? . . . Behold, the Lord God will help me. . . who is he who shall condemn me? Lo, they all shall wax old as a garment; the moth shall eat them up." (Isaiah 50:8-9)

As we seek His face, and His glory, He causes even our enemies to be at peace with us.

I have often gone to the Lord in prayer in times of doubt and uncertainty, and in times when the enemy has unleashed a flood of enemies to attack me, asking Him to restore or increase my faith. I have learned that it is not my faith that needs restoration or increase, but my vision. The enemy does not attack our faith, he attacks our vision.

Scripture tells us that "without a vision, the people perish, or cast off restraint." (Proverbs 29:18) This is why the devil attacks our vision. It is our vision that causes our faith to blossom. The word vision in this passage can mean "prophetic revelation." Revelation 19:10 tells us that "the testimony of Jesus is the spirit of prophesy." In our quest for intimacy with the Father, we must first have intimacy with the Son. As we have intimacy with Jesus, because He is the spirit of prophesy, we gain revelation. It is the revelation of Jesus that causes our vision to expand. Once we grasp hold of a vision greater than our natural ability to accomplish, we are assured the only way it can come to pass is by the hand of God. The vision, or prophetic revelation, God imparted to Moses when He spoke from within the burning bush was to go and tell Pharaoh, "Let my people go." Moses' response was "Who am I that you should send me?" (Exodus 3:11)

God gave Moses a big vision. A vision that was too big for him to accomplish out of his own strength, and he knew it. When you feel your faith is at it lowest, seek the Lord and ask Him to enlarge your vision. As the breadth and depth of your vision increases, so, too, will your faith increase.

What is the final result of dwelling, or abiding, with the Lord in Hebron?

The kingdom is united, and Jerusalem, becomes our capital. "So all the elders of Israel came to the king to Hebron; and king David made a league with them in Hebron before the Lord: and they anointed him king over Israel . . . In Jerusalem he reigned thirty and three years over all Israel and Judah. (2Samuel 5:3,5) When we dwell spiritually in Hebron, we come into unity, not only with the Lord, but with one another. Our united capital is Jerusalem—the place of peace. This is true and lasting unity–a unity born of the Spirit of God, not from the souls of men. It cannot be corrupted, or tarnished. It brings with it spiritual power and authority. The same authority Jesus walked in as a man.

Many voices today call for unity in the body, but they attempt to birth unity out of a "works" mentality. Programs will never bring true and lasting unity. Dwelling in the cities of praise (Judah), gaining intimacy with the Father through the Son, beholding the glory of the Lord, abiding in His magnificent Presence, this is what brings unity.

Notice that it was the elders of Israel, the leadership, *who came to David* in Hebron. He did not command them to come. He did not demand they come. He simply heard and obeyed. God did the rest. "And David perceived that the Lord had established him king over Israel, and that He had exalted his kingdom *for His people Israel's sake.*" (2Samuel 5:12) (Italics mine.)

It is God, and God alone, who brings unity to the Body of Christ, and He does so *for His people's sake.* Our task is to endeavor to hear His Voice, and then obey His commands. Jesus said, "The Son can do nothing of Himself, but what He sees the Father do . . ." (John 5:19)

It is then that Jesus will openly manifest Himself to us.

It is then we will see His glory.

The Living Torah

—ᴍ—

A nyone who has been a Christian for more than a few weeks
is familiar with John 1:1: **In the beginning was the Word,
and the Word was with God, and the Word was God.** We learn
from Revelation 19:13 that Jesus is called the Word of God, which
confirms John 1:14, "And the Word was made flesh, and dwelt
among us . . ."

Jesus, then, is the Word of God, incarnate.

But what exactly is meant by the Word of God in this context?
One way to answer that question is to step out of the Greek mindset
and examine the phrase from a Hebraic viewpoint.

Hebrew is called *"LaShon HaKodesh,"* the holy speech of
tongue. Many today believe that when God spoke through the
prophet Zephaniah and said, "For then will I turn to the people a pure
language, that they may all call upon the name of the Lord to serve
Him with one consent," He was speaking of Hebrew as a universal
language. (Zephaniah 3:9) Whether or not this is true remains to be
seen. What is true, however, is that Hebrew is the language of the
Old Testament Scriptures, and therein lies a key for understanding
the phrase "the Word made flesh."

Today, and historically, there are three major areas of study in
Jewish religious training institutions, or *yeshivot*: God, the people of
Israel, and Torah. For our purposes, we shall focus on the Torah. In its
broadest sense Torah embodies all the authoritative teachings of the
rabbis. While it is often referred to as *the Law*, it is more appropriately
defined as simply *teaching*, or *instruction*. Rabbinic Jewish thinking

57

proclaims both an oral and written Torah. The written Torah is typically referred to as the *Chumash*. The Greeks translate it *Pentateuch*, the first five books of the Bible. This Torah was the one written by Moses as he received it from God on Mount Sinai. According to the rabbis, there is also an oral tradition received by Moses which was passed down by word of mouth from Moses to Joshua, from Joshua to the elders, from the elders to the prophets, and from the prophets to the men of the Great Assembly. Eventually, this oral tradition was written down and became the basis for the Talmud, considered to be the most authoritative collection of oral Torah.

The Torah contains all the great theological concepts found throughout the Bible–sin, sacrifice, salvation, sanctification, and the advent of Messiah.

In their excellent work **Torah Rediscovered**, Ariel and D'vorah Berkowitz point out that one of the unique features of the Torah is that it is actually three documents in one. It is a teaching in which God revealed Himself to mankind and taught us about His righteousness. It is also a covenant, a legally binding agreement between God and His chosen people, the Jews. In effect, it is the Jewish National Constitution. Finally, it is also a *ketubah*, a formal written document which elucidates the specific terms of a Jewish marriage contract.

This is why the Torah is often referred to as "the book of covenant." Israel is the bride, and God is the groom. Mount Sinai is the site of the wedding, and God's *Shekinah* Glory is the *chuppah*, or covering, over the ceremony.

The Torah, then, is much more than simply "the Law." It is a profound document with far- reaching implications. We are told in Romans 3:20 that the Torah educates us to the knowledge of sin, in Romans 4:15 that the Torah brings about the wrath of God, and in Galatians 3:23 that the Torah is our protector. Simply put, the Torah contains judgments, commandments, and ordinances. In this sense, it is indeed "the Law."

However, the legal aspect of Torah, in its purest sense, was not given by God as a set of laws and commands to be obeyed in order to secure, or earn, His righteousness. Rather, the Torah should be viewed more appropriately as a hedge of protection for those who obey its tenets and commands, until such time as the advent of Messiah. (Galatians 3:24)

Today, in the Body of Christ, there is tremendous misunderstanding about the true concept of Torah. These various misunderstandings invariably lead to divisions, or schisms, within the Body. Generally, misunderstanding arises wherever the word Torah is translated simply as "the Law." In the broadest sense, conflict arises between individuals who believe it is important that "the Law" be observed or followed, in all its various aspects, and those who argue that we are no longer subject to "the Law" but live under grace because of the death, burial, and resurrection of Jesus.

As in most disputes of this type, there is no right or wrong. Both doctrinal positions are valid, and, surprisingly, not mutually exclusive. The clearest enunciation of this fact comes from The Master Himself:

"Don't think that I have come to abolish the Torah, or the Prophets. I have come not to abolish, but to complete. Yes indeed! I tell you that until heaven and earth pass away, not so much as a *yud* or a stroke will pass from the Torah–not until everything that must happen has happened. So whoever disobeys the least of these *mitzvot* and teaches others to do so will be called the least in the Kingdom of Heaven. But whoever obeys them and so teaches will Be called great in the Kingdom of Heaven. (Matthew 4:17, CJB)

Mitzvot are commandments. Jesus is telling us in this passage that He is the *fulfillment* of the Torah, not its annulment or antithesis. Not surprisingly, some of His earliest followers, all of whom were Jews until approximately eight years after His crucifixion, referred to Him as "*haTorah.*" The Torah! Jesus further admonishes His listeners, who now include us, to keep all His Father's commands and teach others to do so. This does not mean we are bound by a legalistic interpretation of Torah. Far from it. Grace abounds, as the Apostle Paul assures us in his epistle to the church at Rome. But this doesn't mean that we are free to ignore and repudiate the constraints of Torah. (Romans

5:20, 6:1-2) Rather, we are to consider ourselves dead to sin and its power over us, because of the shed blood of Jesus.

We are exhorted to walk in newness of life, because our baptism is not only that of water, but of the baptism of death through the Cross. Because of our identification with His death on the Cross, made possible by the shedding of His Holy and sin-free Blood, "our old man is crucified with Him, that the body of sin might be destroyed, that henceforth we might not serve sin." (Romans 6:6)

When we take the time to read Scripture under the inspiration and tutelage of the Holy Spirit, the imagery contained within it is extraordinarily powerful and life-changing.

In a sense, we can divide an individual's life into three broad categories.

According to Scripture we are all born in sin because of Adam and Eve's transgression. In this state, we are slaves to sin. Even if we desire to "be good," we cannot because of the curse in the Earth. Invariably, we sin. Sadly, many in the world never transition beyond this category.

However, if we choose to accept the Son of God, Jesus, as our Savior, we pass from death to life in Him. We are translated out of the kingdom of darkness into the kingdom of light. This second category is instant. It occurs, not because of who we are, or what we do, but because of who God is, and what He did. Romans 2:4 tells us it is "the goodness of God that leads men to repentance." He loves us first that we might love Him. When we respond to His Love, we become a new creation. Over time, old things pass away, everything becomes new.

Not only that, but something extraordinary, something mystical happens.

Paul writes to the Corinthians and says, ". . . you are the temple of the living God; as God has said, I will dwell in them, and walk in them; and I will be their God, and they shall be my people." (2Corinthians 6:16) This is nothing less than God fulfilling the covenant He made with Abraham, Moses, David, and others. When God gave Moses, and the nation of Israel, the Ten Commandments, He wrote the Torah on tablets of stone. Yet, through His prophet

Jeremiah, approximately six hundred and fifty years before the birth of Christ, He promised His chosen people the following:

"Here, the days are coming," says *Adonai*, "when I will make a new covenant with the house of Israel and with the house of *Y'huda* [Judah]. It will not be like the covenant I made with their fathers on the day I took them by their hand and brought them out of the land of Egypt; because they, for their part, violated my covenant, even though I, for My part, was a husband to them," says *Adonai*."For this is the covenant I will make with the house of Israel after those days," says *Adonai*. I will put my Torah within them and write it on their hearts; I will be their God, and they shall be my people. (Jeremiah 31:32-33, CJB)

God also spoke through His prophet Ezekiel and told his chosen people that He was going to give Israel a new heart. He promised to put a new spirit within them, get rid of their stony heart, and give them instead a heart of flesh. Then, because of this miraculous transformation, they would walk in His statutes and ordinances and possess the land promised to Abraham. (Ezekiel 11:19-20, 36:25-28).

In both the Jeremiah and Ezekiel passages, God clearly alludes to the Torah, His Law. After God delivered His people out of the hand of pharaoh, and bondage, He gave them, through Moses, the Torah at Mount Sinai. The Law was then written in stone. This was His visible, written covenant with Israel, His *ketuba*. However, His true desire was to have His Torah written in their hearts. The only way this could be done was for Messiah to come to Earth, live as a man, walk among us, die, and be resurrected. This was the way God intended to give His people a new spirit, and transform their hearts of stone into hearts of flesh. So it is with those of us who accept Christ as our Savior, by faith. He transforms our stony hearts into hearts of flesh. He has written His Torah, His Law, on our hearts.

The third category is that of choosing, on a daily basis, to go to Gethsemane. There, we die to self, so that we might be able to take up the cross of Christ. Each of us has different things in our soul which remain as stumbling blocks to intimacy with the Father, even after salvation. While it's true that redemption, in the sense of being born into the kingdom of light, is instant, it is also progressive. The goal of this process is that by yielding ourselves to the Holy Spirit, our souls—that is, our mind, will, and emotions—are renewed in the image and likeness of Christ. This is the process of overcoming the world.

The prize is beyond measure.

We who overcome are promised by God that He will once again allow us to eat from the tree of life (Revelation 2:7), that we will not be hurt by the second death (Revelation 2:11), that we will have power over all the nations (Revelation 2:26), that our names will be written in the Book of Life (Revelation 3:5), that we will become pillars in the Temple of God, and His name shall be written upon us (Revelation 3:12), that we will sit with Messiah Jesus in the Throne of God (Revelation 3:21), and that we will be called sons of God, entitled to inherit all things. (Revelation 21:7)

It is through this process of dying to those things which our soul desires, those idols which enslave us—because our ancestors ate from the Tree of the Knowledge of Good and Evil and thus contaminated the bloodline of humanity—that we become lights set upon a hill, shining forth into a darkened world. Prior to salvation, sin was our master. We bowed to its demands, because we could not possibly will to do otherwise. When we accept Christ, we gain the ability not only to flee sin, but to *resist* it.

The imagery in the book of Psalms regarding sin is that of "falling into a trap set by a fowler." (Psalm 91:3) As a new creation, we are trapped, or ensnared, by sin whenever we stray out of the protection of the Most High God. As long as we stay hidden in the shadow of His wings, we are able to resist temptation, and thus keep from falling into sin. Where is the shadow of his wings? The Ark of the Covenant. The Most Holy Place. The Secret Place of the Most High God.

The Cleft of the Rock.

We will talk more about this in the final chapter, **His Precious Blood.**

The Apostle James tells us there are three stages to sin. First, we are tempted. The place we are tempted is in those areas of our soul where we have not allowed the Lord to redeem us. Yet, it is not simply being enticed by our own lusts which precipitates our downfall. There is a measure of enchantment, or beguilement, which intensifies the temptation. This is what happened to Eve in the Garden of Eden. The next step, after enticement, is conception. Sin is not instant. It is birthed. When we give place to temptations by dwelling upon them in our minds, we literally water and fertilize sin. Finally, when sin has run its full course, when we have acted out what we previously only thought about, death gains a small measure of victory over us. (James 1:14-15)

Left unchecked, the spirit of Death takes a horrific, cumulative toll.

Beloved, every time we succumb to a temptation, we risk a measure of death in our lives. And the death that God is most concerned about is not the death of our flesh, but the death of our soul. All flesh is as grass and the goodness it produces is like a flower that fades away. It is only the Word of God which lasts forever. (Isaiah 40:6-8) The Word of God is Jesus. It is this Word in us—Jesus in us by the power of the Holy Spirit—that sustains us, and gives us the ability to resist temptation. If we resist, and endure, we are promised the crown of life. (James 1:10)

How do we do this?

How do we resist and overcome temptation?

At the time of Jesus there were primarily two political groups of religious Jews–the Pharisees and Sadducees. The Pharisees were legalists. They were quick to condemn all, even other Jews, who failed in their eyes to keep every "jot and tittle" of the Torah. Yet Jesus rebuked them, and the scribes, for their behavior, saying, "Woe unto you, scribes and Pharisees, hypocrites, for you are like whitened sepulchers, which indeed appear beautiful outwardly, but are within full of dead men's bones and of all uncleanness. Even so you also outwardly appear righteous unto men, but within you are full of hypocrisy and iniquity." (Matthew 23:27-28)

Jesus obviously had a very different attitude about the importance of the Torah in the everyday life of the people.

It is clear from Scripture that legalism is motivated by a religious spirit. This spirit controls and manipulates others by accusing any who fall short of perfection. Pride is the stronghold that allows the religious spirit to operate, and jealousy is its brick and mortar. Nowhere in Scripture does God command, or expect, perfection. He does command and expect respect, holy fear, reverence, obedience, praise, and worship. This is why Paul instructs the Corinthians that they were not to think of themselves as self-sufficient in anything, but to acknowledge that their sufficiency was in God alone.

Once we accept that faith in our own sufficiency breeds contempt for others who do not conform to our standards or doctrines, we can then truly acknowledge that the only thing we have to offer of eternal value is "Christ in us, the hope of glory." It is then we become ministers, or ambassadors, of a covenant based upon the freedom found in the grace of God, not in the letter of "the Law." (2Corinthians 3:5-6)

The Torah was intended by God to be a kind of spiritual Rosetta Stone. The Rosetta Stone, discovered in seventeen ninety-nine, was a stone slab inscribed with both Greek words and Egyptian hieroglyphics. It made possible the translation of the ancient Egyptian language. This in turn led to an understanding of Egyptian daily life and culture, religion, and politics. Similarly, the Torah was given to the Israelites by God so they might know how to properly relate to Him, how to find prosperity in the land that He promised them, and how to share the knowledge of Him with all the nations of the earth so that they too might prosper. Further, it was intended by God to be a sort of temporary tutor until the advent of Messiah.

The Torah reveals spiritual realities which have eternal impact and consequences. Some Jewish mystics go so far as to suggest that the universe was created *out of* and *using* the Torah. They believe the very fabric of the universe is the Torah. This is not a foreign concept to believers in Jesus the Messiah. In both the Book of Colossians and the Book of Hebrews we are told that not only was the universe created by, and for, Jesus, but that He upholds all things "by the word of His power." (Colossians 1:16; Hebrews 1:3)

We see very clearly the process by which this was accomplished in the Book of Genesis.

When the oral tradition of the Jews became the written Word in the time of Ezra, there was not formal punctuation as there is today. The modern Bible as we read it now consists of an arbitrary structure known as books, chapters, and verses. In early Hebrew and Greek writings, punctuation was accomplished not by sentence or paragraph breaks, but by word placement and emphasis. Of particular interest is the creation story.

In Genesis 1:1 through Genesis 2:3 the phrase "and God said" is used ten times. Numerically, ten signifies the perfection of divine order. Some obvious examples are The Ten Commandments, the ten plagues on Egypt, the ten kingdoms of the anti-Christ's world power, the ten trials of Abraham's faith, the parable of the ten virgins, and so on.

The Hebrew word translated God in these scriptures is *Elohim*, the plural form of *Eloh*. Paradoxically, even though a plural noun is used, the verb tense is always singular. This grammatical oxymoron is a very persuasive argument for the representation of the Trinity from the very first verse of the Bible.

However, beginning in Genesis 2:4 the phrase "the Lord God" is used. In Hebrew, it is *Adonai Elohim*. This phrase is used from Genesis 2:4 through Genesis 4:24 in respect to the creation of the earth and heavens, the formation of man, the planting of the Garden of Eden, the taking of Eve from Adam's side, the banishment of man from the Garden after The Fall, as well as numerous other creative acts performed by "the Lord God."

Many assume that the account beginning in Genesis 2:4 is merely a repetitive one, mirroring the initial account of creation. What if something far more profound is occurring in these passages?

We read in Hebrews 11:1 that faith is the substance of things hoped for, the evidence of things not seen. Perhaps what we are being told in Genesis 2:4 is that God the Father commanded, "Let there be Light," and God the Son created the Light out of the "substance" of Faith, using the power of God, the Holy Spirit. We read in 1 Corinthians 12:4-6, "Now there are diversities of gifts, but the same Spirit. And there are differences of administrations, but the same Lord. And there are diversities of operations, but the same God which works in all." God the Father commanded, Jesus the Son administered, or created, God the Holy Spirit was the power, or gifting. Operations, administrations, and giftings—all working together, in unity and harmony—created, made, and formed the universe, and all that is in it.

It was Jesus, in His pre-incarnate existence, who did the actual work of creation.

He formed the worlds.

He created the Light.

He did it all.

Man was formed and created in the image and likeness of God, or better, Jesus. Scripture reveals that Jesus was the "last Adam" and was a "quickening spirit," while the original Adam was made a living soul. (1Corinthians 15:45) We know Jesus was the express image of God, the firstborn of every creature. The Greek words used in Colossians 1:15 to describe Him as such have the connotation of a king using his ring to imprints his seal in molten wax. The resulting image is an identical representation. All who saw the seal would know which king had put his imprint into the wax. There could be no mistake, because the seal was an exact waxen replica of the king's ring.

Jesus was, and is, the express image of God.

This is why He told Philip that any who had seen Him had seen The Father. (John14:6-9) Jesus was, and is, the Torah made *flesh*. Jesus was, and is, the *Living* Torah. And we are His creation. His brethren. We are adopted into His family, the household of faith, by virtue of His shed blood, and His resurrection. This is what the Apostle John refers to when he writes, "But as many as received Him, to them gave He power to become the sons of God, even to them that believe on His name: Which were born not of blood, nor of the will of the flesh, nor of the will of man, but of God." (John 1:12-13)

Jesus is called the Word of God. He is also called the True Light. God is Light and in Him there is no darkness. The spiritual realm is Light. The Bible talks about the Kingdom of Light, versus the Kingdom of Darkness.

Jesus was the *Word* made flesh.

The *Torah* made flesh.

Light made flesh.

Historically, the Jews have referred to the visible manifestation of the brightness or Glory or God as "the *Shekinah*." Although not specifically mentioned in the Bible, there are repeated references to the *Shekinah* of God in extra-Biblical Hebrew writings. The

Biblical term is the Glory of God. *Shekinah* literally means *"the one who dwells."* The inference, of course, is that it is God who visibly dwells among His people. In Judaic tradition it was told that the burning lamps outside the veil of the Holy of Holies were a sign that the *Shekinah*, or visible presence of the Lord, resided in Israel.

The first reference to this visible manifestation of the Glory of God is found in the account of the Exodus. The Glory manifested as a pillar of cloud by day and a pillar of fire by night. (Exodus 13:21) Both of these manifestations of the Glory were clearly witnessed by over a million people. We are also told that the Lord came down in the pillar of cloud. (Numbers 12:5) When the Tabernacle of Moses was completed, the first thing that happened was the Glory of God, the *Shekinah*, descended upon it. At that time, the weight of God's Glory was so strong, not even Moses could enter the Tabernacle. (Exodus 40:34-35)

It is interesting to see the progressive imagery set forth in the design and construction of the Tabernacle, as it relates to the Glory of God. The Outer Court, accessible to all Jews, derived its light from the Sun and Moon. In other words, natural light. The Inner Court, accessible only to the priests, was lighted by seven lamp stands. Seven, of course, is the number of spiritual perfection. The Psalmist tells us that "The words of *Adonai* are pure words, silver in a melting pot set in the earth, refined and purified seven times over." (Psalm 12:6, CJB) These seven lamp stands may well have represented the seven spirits of God–the Spirit of the Lord, the Spirit of wisdom, and understanding, the Spirit of counsel, and might, the Spirit of knowledge, and of the fear of the Lord. (Isaiah 11:2; Revelation 3:1, 5:6)

Jesus was all of these, and more.

It is also likely that they represented the divine calling of the Israelites, to whom pertains the adoption, and the Glory, and the covenants, and the giving of Torah, and the service of God, and the promises. (Romans 9:4) Perhaps they also represented the seven days of creation. In Hebrew, seven is *"shevah,"* meaning *"to be full or satisfied, having enough of."* God rested on the seventh day of creation, having completed His creations. The word Sabbath also derives from this same root.

The Holy of Holies had no natural or artificial light, yet it was the brightest area of the Tabernacle. Here was the resting place of the Ark of the Covenant. Here, according to Asaph, resided the Shepherd of Israel . . . the One who dwells between the Cherubim and shines forth. (Psalm 80:1) The Glory that rested in, and upon, the Ark was a Light which Timothy said no man could approach, nor had seen, nor can see. (1Timothy 5:15-16)

In time, however, the Lord of Glory Himself left behind His status as God, came to earth, lived as a man, died as a man, and was resurrected, that we might behold His Glory. Light made manifest. Light made flesh. The only begotten Son of God.

It makes perfect sense; yet, it is almost incomprehensible.

Light became flesh.

Physicists tell us that when we turn on a light in a room we do not actually see the light itself. Rather, what we see is the *reflection* of light particles off the physical substance of our world. Were it not for the physical substance that light impacts, we could not see it. Our eyes would perhaps register it, but would not be able to catalog it.

Thus, when Jesus took on the form of man, humanity could now see Light manifested *in human form.*

We, His physical creation, were created and formed to *reflect* His Glory.

This is why we were made in the image and likeness of Him.

If He'd made us anything less, we would not have been capable of reflecting His Light. This is why Scripture teaches us that God "has made us able to be partakers of the inheritance of the saints in light. Who has delivered us from the power of darkness, and has translated us into the kingdom of His dear Son." (Colossians 1:12-13)

God's kingdom is Light.

In Him there is no darkness. No shadow of turning. His thoughts are Light. His breath is Light. His Word is Light. His Son is Light. When the Apostle John writes that the Light shined into the darkness, but the darkness did not comprehend it, he was referring to the minds of men, which have been darkened by the curse of sin.

Jesus clearly states that the foundation of sin is unbelief. (John 16:9) All the sins of mankind stem from this fundamental lack of faith. God is more concerned about our separation from Him, than He is our sin. Sin was dealt with once and for all time at the Cross. But we cannot receive the benefit of His atoning blood if we remain separated from Him. And it is our unbelief that drives a wedge between us and Him.

Prior to the Fall, Adam walked and talked with the Lord in the cool of the day. There was no separation, no estrangement. The Glory of the Lord was his covering. After The Fall, the Glory departed and mankind became separated from its Creator. The Glory didn't manifest again until the Exodus, and then only as a pillar of a cloud, or a pillar of fire. The *Shekinah* came when the Tabernacle of Moses was completed. But that Glory was only temporary. Only the High Priest was allowed to experience it in its fullness, and then only once a year to atone for the sins of the people.

One of the main reasons we cry out so desperately for His Glory to manifest is that when we are in His presence we feel "connected." In His presence, we no longer feel lost and alone. In His presence, nothing can harm us. We also cry out because God puts that desire in our hearts. His character, His very nature, is redemptive. He longs for us to come and abide in His presence that He might restore to us that which we lost in the Garden of Eden.

The Eternal Glory, the Glory without measure, the Glory fully manifested, is Jesus.

The Word made flesh.

The True Light revealed.

The Living Torah.

Resurrection Power

—ᴍ—

In Matthew 24, Levi, son of Alphaeus, brother of James, one of the twelve Apostles, begins his narrative account of the well-known Olivet prophecy. Immediately prior to this, the former tax collector tells us in gripping words that Jesus cried out in anguish over His beloved city, Jerusalem, and prophesied its destruction. Simultaneously, we are told, the Galilean rebuked God's chosen people, His people, the seed of Abraham, for their rebellion. He informed them in no uncertain terms that both the nation of Israel, and the magnificent temple—built by Solomon, destroyed by Nebuchadnezzar, then rebuilt by Zerubbabel and Herod—would be left desolate. Jesus concluded His anguished rebuke with these powerful and prophetic words: "You shall not see Me henceforth until you say, '*Baruch HaBa BaShem Adonai,*' "Blessed is He who comes in the Name of the Lord."

An even more poignant account is recorded in the Gospel of Luke: "And when He (Jesus) was come near, He beheld the city, and wept over it." (Luke 19:41) The Greek word translated "*wept*" in this heart-rending passage is the word" *klaio.*" Literally translated, it means to "*wail in lamentation.*"

What an extraordinary, powerful image!

The Son of God, the Anointed One, the long awaited Messiah of Israel weeps openly before a multitude of people and simultaneously predicts the destruction of God's beloved city and the coming desolation of His chosen people. A stunning event, no doubt. But not nearly as stunning as the only other recorded time that Jesus weeps openly before a large crowd of people.

That occasion involved the death, burial, and resurrection of Lazarus, one of Jesus' closest friends. The passage of two millennia has not diminished the searing imagery of these dramatic moments.

Upon His arrival in Bethany, after the death of Lazarus, Martha rebukes Jesus for not arriving sooner. She tells Him that had He come sooner her brother might still be alive. Jesus responds by telling her that Lazarus will rise again. Martha tells Him she believes her brother will rise in the resurrection—at the last day. Jesus replies that whosoever believes in Him shall never die, and asks her if she believes Him. She responds with, "I believe you are the Christ, the Son of God, who should come into the world." (John 11:21-27)

Sadly, like so many of us today, Martha can't quite bring herself to admit that she believes in the power of Resurrection Life *today*.

But I'm getting ahead of myself.

More about this poignant scene later.

Back to Matthew's account of the Olivet prophesy.

After rebuking the Pharisees, calling them a generation of vipers, and holding them accountable for "all the righteous blood shed upon the earth, from the blood of righteous Abel unto the blood of Zacharias, son of Barachias, whom you slew between the temple and the altar," and grieved by what He has seen His Father's house, the Temple, become—a den of thieves, a haven for moneychangers, a holy place now defiled—Jesus departs the city.

Accompanied by Peter, James, John, and Andrew, he climbs the Mount of Olives.

No insignificant place, this mile long ridge of limestone over-looks Jerusalem, and the Temple. It was from here, earlier in his ministry, that Jesus made His triumphal entry into the city. Then, He was sitting astride a donkey as it walked along the dusty road that winds its way from Bethany, around the southern shoulder of the Mount, through the massive outer gates, into the city proper. In His heart He knew that in a very short time He would make the climb up to Gethsemane, the garden known to all as the place where olives were pressed to extract their precious oil. One wonders if He also knew that it would be a climb up to one of the most agonizing and singularly powerful moments of His entire time on earth. For it was here that the Son of Man wrestled for three hours with His soul, agonizing over His final, inevitable choice—

The Cross.

Later, after his death, burial, and resurrection, it was from here that He ascended to His Father in Heaven. Triumphant. Victorious. "[T]he head of the body, the church: who is the beginning, the first-born from the dead; that in all things He might have the preeminence. For it pleased the Father that in Him should all fullness dwell. And having made peace through the blood of His cross, by Him to recon-cile all things unto Himself . . ." (Colossians 1:18-20)

But now, as Jesus and four of his disciples looked out over the city, and the Temple below them, the only man in history to heal the sick and raise the dead had other things on his mind.

The disciples questioned the man they'd called Rabbi, teacher, for nearly three years. "Tell us," they asked, "when shall these things be, and when shall be the sign of your coming . . . and of the end of the age."

Before answering their questions directly, Jesus issued a prophetic warning to the four disciples who had followed Him faith-fully: "Take heed that no man deceive you. For many shall come in my name saying, I am Christ; and shall deceive many . . ." (Matthew 24:4-5) The Gospel of Luke adds a further, powerful admonishment: ". . . go you not therefore after them." (Luke 21:8)

This is not the only warning to the Apostles. Later in the same discourse, Jesus said, ". . . if any man shall say unto you, Lo, here is Christ, or there; believe not. For there shall arise false Christs, and false prophets, and shall show signs and wonders; insomuch that *if it were possible* they shall deceive the very elect. (Italics mine)

Why is it that Jesus believed it necessary to warn his disciples, and us, about false Christs?

Part of the answer is found in Revelation 12:9. The Apostle John, writing from the isle of Patmos during his time of captivity there, having been imprisoned by the Emperor Domitian some sixty-two years after the crucifixion, tells of a mighty war in Heaven. Michael and his angels fight against the dragon and his angels. And the dragon loses. (Revelation 2:7-8) John then writes, "And the great dragon was cast out (of heaven), that old serpent, called the Devil, and Satan, *which deceives the world.*" (Italics mine) The architect of deception is God's adversary, the Great Liar, *Ha-Satan* in the Hebrew, which means "the accuser."

But, some say, "I certainly would never knowingly serve Satan. Indeed, I would recognize him immediately, because he is evil, and I want no part of evil. I am a good person and I desire only to do good things." Yet, the Apostle Paul warns us about "false apostles, deceitful workers" who "transform themselves into the apostles of Christ." (2Corinthians 11:13) Paul goes on to say that we shouldn't be surprised by this type of deceptive masquerade because, "Satan himself is transformed into an angel of light. Therefore, it is no great thing if his ministers also be transformed as the ministers of righteousness."(v. 14-15)

A more practical, less esoteric, warning about the earthly reality of deception is given in Romans 16:17-18. There, Paul writes, "Now I beseech you brethren, mark them which cause divisions and offenses *contrary to the doctrine which you have learned; and avoid them.* For they that are such serve not the Lord, but their own belly; and by *good words* and *fair speeches* deceive the hearts of the simple." (Italics mine)

The imagery here is of an intentional misrepresentation by one skilled in the art of beguiling the unwary, or ignorant. The word *simple* used in this passage does not mean stupidity, but rather having a lack of knowledge of the truth. We would do well to hearken unto the prophetic words of Hosea, uttered to the Israelites in the Seventh Century B.C.. Even today, they strike a cord that should ring in our ears: "My people perish for lack of knowledge . . ." (Hosea 4:6)

What was Paul referring to in Romans 16:17 when he spoke of "the doctrine which you have learned"? And why is this doctrine a stumbling block to the unbeliever? The answer can be found in 1 Corinthians 1:18-25:

For the preaching of the cross is to them that perish, foolishness; but unto us which are saved it is the power of God . . .

For the Jews require a sign, and the Greeks seek after wisdom: But we preach Christ crucified, unto the Jews a stumbling block, and unto the Greeks, foolishness.

But unto them which are called, both Jews and Greeks, Christ the power of God, and the wisdom of God. Because the foolishness of God is wiser than men; and the weakness of God is stronger than men.

Why is it that preaching Christ crucified stirs up so much debate? One can go to a social gathering of unbelievers and talk about anything from AIDS, to abortion, to politics, without fear of censorship. But mention one Name and the atmosphere changes dramatically.

Why?

Because after the crucifixion came *The Resurrection.*

And it is the Resurrection Power of the shed blood of Jesus that is unique in all the history of the world. It is unique in the history of all the world's religions — those that have come and gone, and those that remain to this day.

There is no question that Resurrection Power is what makes Christianity stand alone among all the religions of the world. None of the great spiritual leaders or prophets of any other religion, in any other period of history, have ever claimed to be *The* Son of God. Of all those throughout history who have claimed to represent God, in whatever form, none, save Jesus, has ever been raised from the dead. Further, the historical veracity of the existence of Jesus of Nazareth is not in doubt. There are too many non-Biblical records which support the Biblical account for that to be the case. What is argued, however, is the veracity of Resurrection Power. Why? Because the concept of being raised from the dead, both physically and spiritually, not only confounds the best intellects the world has ever produced, but it is the lifeblood of Christianity.

Witness the conversation between Jesus and one of the most prominent Pharisees the first century, and one of three richest men in Jerusalem — Nicodemus. Interestingly, his name in Greek means *victor over the people.*

Nicodemus was a highly respected member of the Sanhedrin, and as such he wielded much power. He, like all Pharisees of his day believed in the concept of resurrection from the dead *at the last day.* Remember Martha's words to Jesus after the death of her brother, Lazarus? Like Martha, the concept of resurrection power happening *today*, at the command of a man who claimed to be the Son of God, was too much for Nicodemus to grasp, in spite of all his earthly knowledge.

Nicodemus, having heard of some of the more radical teachings of this itinerant carpenter's son, sought out Jesus under the cover of darkness, fearful that he might heap scorn, or worse, upon his head from his fellow members of the Sanhedrin if they knew of his genuine interest in what Jesus had to say.

When he finally encountered Jesus, Nicodemus, no doubt, had the same question in his mind that other skeptical Jews had been asking: What sign would this man Jesus show to prove that He was indeed the Son of God, as those close to Him claimed He was? But Nicodemus was a crafty, astute individual. Instead of asking his question directly, he chose instead to frame the question that burned in his heart as a statement, perhaps hoping, as others before him had hoped, to trap Jesus. "Rabbi," he said, "we know that you are a teacher come from God, for no man can do these miracles that you do, except God be with him."

Jesus knew what was in Nicodemus' mind. More importantly, Jesus knew what was in his heart. He was well aware that the response He'd given to the true question on an earlier occasion, "Destroy this temple, and in three days I will raise it up," would likely be as misunderstood now, even as it had been then. Why? Because Nicodemus, like the Jews who'd questioned Him earlier, was thinking "carnally" (Romans 8:6) and would no doubt believe that He was talking about the *earthly* temple. When, in fact, He was talking about the temple of the living God. (1Corinthians 6:19-20)

Therefore, instead of addressing the question Nicodemus verbalized, Jesus responded to his unasked question with a statement that caught this man of wealth and power totally off guard. "Verily, verily I say unto you, Except a man be born again, he cannot see the kingdom of God." (John 3:1-3)

Nicodemus was astonished by the reply. He pressed Jesus to explain. "How can a man be born when he is old?" he asked incredulously. "And how can he enter his mother's womb a second time to be born again?"

Jesus' rebuke was swift, and pointed. However, His intention was to bring enlightenment, not ridicule: "Are you a master of Israel, and know you not these things . . .? Verily, verily I say unto you, We speak that we do know, and testify that we have seen; and you receive not our witness. If I have told you earthly things, and you believe not, now shall you believe if I tell you heavenly things?" (John 3:10-12)

We would do well, both individually and corporately as the Body, to heed these important words of our Savior and Lord. One of the greatest failings of the modern Church has been to allow the doctrine of The Resurrection to become something that, for the most part, is only preached once a year. And it is rarely taught in its entirety. Consequently, few Christians truly embrace all the fullness that Resurrection Life offers. Like Martha, their doctrine is one of believing that Christ will raise them up at the *Last Day*. But on a day-to-day basis, their lives are not resurrected. Because of this, they are unable, or worse, unwilling, to take up their crosses and die daily.

What does it mean to live our lives believing wholly in the power of resurrection?

It means we truly believe that we are "bought with a price" and that we are not to be "the servants of men." (1Corinthians 7:23) The primary way we find ourselves serving man instead of God is out of fear. Inculcating the fear of man versus the fear of God is one of the enemy's chief weapons. He uses the fear of man to keep us from accomplishing that which God has ordained in our lives, and he perverts the fear of God by using men to distort the meaning of the phrase.

The first instance where the phrase "fear of God" is used in the Bible is in Genesis 20:11. During his wandering, Abraham encounters Abimelech, king of Gerar, a Philistine city situated on the border between Israel and Egypt. Abimelech is smitten by Sarah, Abraham's half sister, and his wife. Fearful the king will kill him, Abraham offers Sarah to Abimelech. However, God gives the innocent king a dream in which He tells Abimelech that Sarah is Abraham's wife and commands the king to restore Sarah to her rightful husband. God's command is quite forceful. He tells the king that if he restores Sarah, he will live, but if he fails to obey God's command, not only will he die, but all his family as well. To his credit, Abimelech obeys God and not only restores Sarah to Abraham, but gives the wandering Jew a thousand pieces of silver, along with sheep, oxen, and both men and women servants. He also tells Abraham that he may pick any place to live in the land of Gerar that he chooses.

What an incredible turn of events.

Abraham gives his wife to a strange man because he is afraid of being killed. Then, the man not only restores his wife, but gives him a tremendous bounty.

What is going on?

The key lies in Abraham's response to the king when he is called before him to account for his behavior. Abimelech asks Abraham, "How have I offended you that you have brought such a great sin upon me and my kingdom?" Abraham replies, "Because I thought, Surely the fear of God is not in this place; and they will slay me for my wife's sake." (Genesis 20: 9-11) Abraham knew about the fear of God. He'd experienced it firsthand on many occasions. When God first spoke to him and commanded him to leave his father's house, when God spoke to him and promised him the land of Canaan, when God spoke to him and promised him not only a son, but said that he would be the father of many nations, and of course, when he negotiated with the Lord to save Sodom and Gomorrah. Yet, in spite of all this, Abraham succumbed to the fear of man. Had God not intervened, Abraham would have lost all.

Beloved, the fear of man will rob us of the promises of God, but the fear of God will insure that God intervenes on our behalf, no matter how dismal the circumstances. Proverbs 1:7 tells us that "the fear of the Lord is the beginning of wisdom," and Proverbs 29:25 warns us that "the fear of man brings a snare." Do not allow the fear of man to keep you from your rightful inheritance. It is said of Abraham that he believed in God, and God counted it to him for righteousness. (Genesis 15:6) If we fear anything, we must fear the

Lord. His judgments are pure and right and designed to draw us closer to Him.

We will examine this concept in depth in a separate chapter entitled **Abiding in Him.**

Paul tells us that pressing toward the mark for the prize of the high calling of God means that our desire should be to ". . . know Him, and the power of His resurrection, and the fellowship of His sufferings," that we might, on an ongoing basis, be made "conformable unto His death." (Philippians 3:10) Knowing God intimately is but the first part of an ongoing process. Knowing Him as God is important and foundational, but even more important is to know the power of His resurrection. We do this, among other ways, by becoming part of the fellowship of His sufferings. This results in our being made conformable unto His death.

The death of the Cross.

Why is it so important that we not only comprehend the significance of the power of His resurrection, but that we walk it out daily in our lives as well?

In a word—*Authority.*

Knowing the power of His resurrection and living it on a daily basis gives us spiritual authority. One of the ways we learn to believe in the power of His resurrection and walk in it on a daily basis is by our sufferings. It has been said, however, that suffering alone is not sufficient to insure spiritual authority with our Lord. It is suffering *for* Him, and suffering for Him *well* that brings that kind of authority. I would agree. Many today in the body of Christ cry out for the power of God to manifest. But few are willing to pay the price required to walk in the kind of spiritual authority that allows the power of God to manifest through them in unprecedented ways.

God is sovereign, and He can do what He wills. However, it is clear from Scripture that He consistently chooses to work through men. If we desire for the Lord to work through us in such a way that we have true spiritual authority, we must, as Paul indicates, not only know the Lord intimately, and the power of His resurrection, but we must also know the fellowship of His sufferings.

Resurrection power not only delivers us from physical and spiritual death, it gives us true power. The power to overcome the world.

When Adam and Eve ate of the Tree of the Knowledge of Good and Evil, both physical and spiritual death entered the world. Prior to that, the Spirit of God ruled the hearts of God's magnificent creation. After the Fall, man's soul ascended to the position of authority and ruled over him. Jesus came, in part, to restore the Spirit's rightful authority. Jesus tells us that "in the world you shall have tribulation: but be of good cheer; I have overcome the world." (John 16:33)

Scripture tells us that when we accept Christ as our Savior, old things pass away and all things become new. But the Bible also admonishes us to work out our salvation with fear and trembling. Why? Salvation is a process, not an event. While it's true that we are saved by grace, through faith, and not of our own doing so that none of us can boast, we must still walk out the process of allowing Jesus to become our Lord, as well as our Savior. Jesus came and lived as a man so that He might be an example of how to do this. Hebrews 4 tells us, "Though He were a Son, yet learned He obedience by the things which He suffered; And *being made perfect*, He became the author of eternal salvation unto all that obey Him."(v. 8-9) (Italics mine.)

Certainly no one would suggest that Jesus, as God incarnate, was imperfect. So what is this passage referring to?

The Greek word for perfect here means "complete" or "consummate." It has nothing to with the deity, or infallibility, of Christ. Rather, it speaks to the fact that Jesus walked as man, and suffered as a man, and overcame the world as a man, so that we might follow in His footsteps. What gave Jesus the strength as a man to endure all the rejection, ridicule, hatred, physical and emotional abuse, and betrayal that he suffered, not to mention His time on the Cross?

It was His absolute faith in The Resurrection.

Jesus was in Jerusalem for the Passover, and He visited the Temple. There, he found the moneychangers, and those who sold oxen, sheep, and doves to the faithful desiring to make a sacrifice. He was so incensed by the carnal activity he witnessed, He chased all the merchants from the Temple, admonishing them not to make His Father's house a house of merchandise. The Jews countered His righteous anger by demanding a sign that He had the authority to chastise them. He responded, "Destroy this temple and in three days I will raise it up." (Matthew 2:13-19)

As we saw earlier, Jesus was speaking about the true temple, not the one built by man.

Jesus, God incarnate, knew what lay in store for Him. Yet He willingly chose to suffer as a man so that He might comfort all those who would suffer after Him and, more importantly, so that we would know that it was possible to endure the same kind of sufferings. Yet there is more. Jesus intended that we do more than simply endure. He intended that we be overcomers. And it is our faith in the power of resurrection that enables us to overcome.

The author of Hebrews writes in chapter twelve, "for the joy set before Him, Jesus endured the cross," and that we should not faint in our minds, or grow weary, when we encounter tribulation because we have not yet "resisted unto blood striving against sin."(v. 2-3) We are told that if we endure chastening that God deals with us as sons, but that if we are without chastisement, we are bastards and not sons.(v. 7-8) Further, we are told that God chastises us for our own profit so that we might walk in righteousness and become partakers of His holiness. (v. 10-11) We are admonished not to allow any root of bitterness to spring up within us so that we don't defile ourselves, or others, and we are warned not to sell our birthright, as did Esau, thereby forfeiting our inheritance of God's blessing.(v. 15-17)

It is clear the disciples had a fundamental grasp of these concepts in terms of resurrection power. James tells us to "count it all joy when we fall into diverse temptations." (James 1:2) Peter admonishes us to greatly rejoice in spite of the fact that we are in tribulation because the trial of our faith is "more precious than gold." (1Peter 1:6-7) John writes, "And they overcame him by the blood of the Lamb, and by the word of their testimony, and they loved not their lives unto death." (Revelation 12:11) Matthew, Mark, and Luke all give clear accounts of their faith in the resurrection.

Embracing resurrection power and implementing that faith on a daily basis is what empowers the believer to endure even the most extreme circumstances, and to overcome the world. Without resurrection, Christianity is just another religion. Without resurrection, our suffering is unbearable and meaningless. Without resurrection, there is no hope in eternal life. If the Church, as a body, is to grow and change into that which the Lord desires, we must individually, and corporately, start adopting attitudes and implementing behaviors that spring from a fundamental belief in, and an understanding of, Resurrection Power.

Scripture gives us striking imagery to understand where we are in the process.

Although there are not three types of salvation, there are, perhaps, three aspects.

There is common salvation, spoken about in Jude 3, great salvation spoken about in Hebrews 2:3, and eternal salvation spoken about in Hebrews 5:9.

Jude writes and admonishes us to contend for the Faith, because there are those who are pervert the doctrines of Christ, and deny his deity. The writer of Hebrews first talks of great salvation in terms of remaining steadfast in the faith and not forgetting the truth of what the Lord preached, and then of eternal salvation in the context of suffering and obedience.

Using the physical layout of the Temple, we can see more clearly what is being said.

The Temple, as well as the Tabernacle of Moses, consisted of the Outer Court, the Inner Court, and the Holy of Holies. Anyone who was a Jew could visit the Outer Court. Only priests could visit the Inner Court. And only the High Priest was allowed to enter the Holy of Holies, and then only once a year to atone for the nation's sins.

With the crucifixion, burial, and resurrection of Jesus, the veil was rent once, and for all time. All who call upon the name of the Lord shall be saved. When we confess with our mouth that Jesus is Lord, and believe in our heart that God raised Him from the dead, we are saved. (Romans 10:9)

This is the common salvation.

It is available to all who believe. The key elements of common salvation are: believing that Jesus was the son of God; that He walked among us as a man; and that He was crucified and resurrected. However, once we understand these basic doctrines we must press on, into the Inner Court.

The Inner Court is where sacrifices were performed.

We are no longer called to sacrifice animals and shed their blood for the remission of sin. Rather, our sacrifice is to "mortify the deeds of the flesh" and to put to death those things which take root in our soul and keep us separated from Christ. (Romans 8:13) We are called to put off the old man and put on the new who is renewed in knowledge according to the original pattern God created. (Colossians 3:9-11) It is in the Inner Court where we learn to have faith in the power of resurrection. As we wrestle with our soul and the things of this world which compete for our attention, as we endure sufferings, and endure them well, holding fast to our faith, we are perfected, even as Christ was perfected.

He is there, with us, in the midst of our trial, in the person of the Holy Spirit, to comfort us when we are tempted to fall away. He has the authority to do this, because He was tempted, and resisted. (Hebrews 2:18) In the fire of our temptation, in the heat of our sufferings, it is our faith in the power of resurrection that sustains us. And it is Resurrection Power that brings us through the fire, so that we can say, as did the Psalmist, "For you, O God, has proved us: You have tried us as silver. You brought us into the net; you laid affliction at our loins. You caused men to ride over our heads: we went through fire and water: but You brought us out into a wealthy place." (Psalm 66:10-12)

This is great salvation. Holding firm to our faith in the midst of trial and tribulation, remembering and living out the truths that Jesus preached.

From the Inner Court we move into the Holy of Holies.

God beckons us to come into His Presence. Deep calls unto deep. We are ushered into His Presence as we trust and obey. Because of the death and resurrection of His Son, Jesus, we can come boldly to the throne of grace and find mercy and grace to help in our time of need. (Hebrews 4:16) In the Holy of Holies we abide in the Presence of a Holy God. In His Presence we behold His Glory. In His presence we are truly transformed, because He is the firstborn of many.

God's desire is that every believer should experience this level of intimacy with Him. Nevertheless, Scripture tells us that many are called, but few are chosen. (Matthew 20:16) This pertains not only to salvation, but to intimacy as well.

Now, back to the story of Jesus and Lazarus.

Martha tells Jesus she believes her brother will be raised in the final resurrection, and then leaves and seeks out her sister, Mary. She tells Mary that Jesus has arrived in Bethany. Mary, in turn, seeks out Jesus and falls at his feet weeping, saying she knows that had He been present, her brother would not have died.

She has faith in Jesus as the Healer, but what about her faith in Him as the Deliverer?

Jesus sees her weeping, and the weeping of the other Jews who were with her. The Bible says He "groaned in the spirit, and was troubled." (John 11:33) There was consternation among the crowd. Some wondered aloud why this man who opened blind eyes did not come sooner and heal Lazarus. Jesus hears their musings and, again, Scripture tells us He groaned in the spirit.

The Jews thought Jesus was groaning because He loved Lazarus like a brother, and Lazarus was now dead. But is that really why Jesus was groaning?

Perhaps not.

The crowd, including Mary and Martha, arrives at the grave. Lazarus has been dead for four days. Jesus says to Martha, "I have said unto that if you would believe you would see the glory of God." He then lifts up His eyes to Heaven and thanks His Father in advance saying, "I thank You that You have heard Me. And I know that you hear me always: but because of the people which stand by I said it, that they might believe that You have sent me." And then he said, "Lazarus, come forth!" (John 11:37-43)

Jesus was making a powerful statement here.

He healed the sick, opened blind eyes, and proclaimed that He came to set the captives free. Yet the most crucial part of His ministry is not healing. It is Resurrection Power—both physical and spiritual. Without resurrection power, healing is only temporary. It affects only the physical body. But what about the soul? Jesus is more interested in the eternal things of the spirit than the temporary things of the flesh. This doesn't mean He isn't compassionate about the immediate physical needs of people, or even the death of one of His closest friends, but rather that His emphasis is on eternity.

Raising Lazarus from the dead was a foreshadowing of what was to come.

Christ's own resurrection.

Jesus groaned in the spirit, because He deeply desired for the people to grasp the essential truth of His ministry. He is the Resurrection and the Life, and all who believe in Him, though they are dead, yet shall they live. This is why He commands the people to "loose Lazarus and let him go." He wants them to be *involved* in what He is doing. He wants them to *believe*.

It is not enough to simply know *about* the Word.

It is not enough to simply know *about* Jesus.

If we truly desire to have old things pass away and all things become new, if we truly desire to have spiritual authority, if we truly desire to see the Glory of God manifested in our lives on a daily basis, we must not only believe in Resurrection Power, we must walk it out daily. This is what it means not to be conformed to this world, but to be transformed by the renewing of our minds. (Romans 12:2)

All authority comes from God. Jesus is the only begotten Son of God. Yet, He came and lived among us as a man. *Everything Jesus did on Earth, He did as a man.* What made Jesus different, was not just his deity, it was His faith in, and obedience to, God. He left his exalted position as God, walked among us as a man, and came to demonstrate to us that the key to walking in Everlasting Life on a daily basis is seeking, hearing, believing, and, most important of all, obeying. We are told to seek, so that we can find. (Matthew 7:7) We are repeatedly commanded that if we have ears to hear, let us hear. (Matthew 11:15; Mark 7:16; Luke 8:8). We are encouraged that when we believe, all things are possible. (Mark 9:23) We are instructed to have the faith of God. (Mark 11:22) And we are admonished to take every thought captive to the obedience of Christ. (2Corinthians 10:5)

If, and when, we do all these things, the Glory of God will manifest in ways that we have only dreamed.

Resurrection Power is what sets Christianity apart from all other religions. However, in order to receive the full benefit of the power that raised Jesus from the dead, we must allow it to be more than simply a religious doctrine we ascribe to.

Our faith in resurrection power must become a living, tangible thing in our lives before it will ever truly transform us.

Once *we* are transformed, we can then transform the world.

Job's Heart

—ш—

The story of Job is a familiar one.

Scripture tells us he was perfect and upright, that he feared God, and that he avoided evil. Satan presented himself before God and claimed the only reason Job exhibited these characteristics was because God had placed a hedge of protection around him, and because God had abundantly blessed him with material things. God responds to the devil and tells him that he has permission take all Job's material possessions from him, including his offspring, but he cannot take his life. The devil rises to the challenge and does what he does best–steal, kill, and destroy. Although Job suffers horribly, he still maintains his faith and confidence in God. He says, "Though He slay me, yet will I trust in Him: but I will maintain mine own ways before Him." (Job 13:15)

It is one thing to suffer calamity because of sin, entirely another to suffer because God allows it as part of His refining process.

We spoke in the chapter on Resurrection Power that because of original sin, all who are born into the Earth suffer. And we saw that it is not simply suffering that builds the kind of character that God desires in us, but suffering for the cause of Christ, and suffering for Him well that truly refines us.

What is extraordinary about Job is that he went through his trials without the benefit of written scripture to help him, without the aid of godly friends, without even a prophetic word to sustain him during in his pain and suffering. All he had was a personal connection with God. For much of his trial, he felt as if even that was cut off. Yet, because of Job's response to his circumstances, because he not only endured but overcame, the Apostle James calls him a prophet of God. (James 5:10-11)

It is clear from Job 31 that the afflictions that came upon Job were not because of sin. Rather, they were part of God's refining process.

Those of us who truly seek the Manifest Presence of God, His Glory, who truly desire to abide in His Presence, who long to see the Body of Christ grow up into its full stature, might as well decide right here and now that we are going to live a life that has a good measure of suffering in it. We must also ask ourselves if our suffering conforms to Colossians 1:24: "I now rejoice in my sufferings for you, and fill up in my flesh what is lacking in the afflictions of Christ, for the sake of His body, which is the church." In other words, are we suffering according to the will of God? (1Peter 4:19)

It is our suffering, and our trials, that produces patience in us. When patience has been fully formed in us by the Master Potter, we reach a level of maturity that makes it possible for Him to use us in ways we only dream about. (James 1:2-4) When we genuinely cry out for the Glory of God to manifest, we are really giving God permission to turn up the heat in our lives. His Presence burns away all that is not of Him. He increases, and we decrease. He transforms us by renewing our minds so that we can begin, in measure, to think like He thinks. His ways are indeed higher than our ways, but because we have His Holy Spirit living inside of us, we can corporately have the mind of Christ. This is a mystery, especially to the unregenerate mind. To those who do not understand, it is utter foolishness to think and believe that God lives inside of men.

No one wants to suffer.

Yet, it seems a false doctrine, a doctrine of men, has crept into the Body of Christ.

That doctrine distorts Scripture and says, among other things, that God intends for us to never be sick, that all of us should be prosperous, and that it is our faith, or lack of it, that determines whether or not we are healthy, wealthy, and wise. It is clear from Scripture this is not the case. Again and again and again we have examples of godly individuals suffering for the cause of Christ, and ultimately being rewarded.

Abraham and Sarah desired children. God promised Abraham that not only would he have a son, but that he would be the "father of many nations." Yet he had to wait twenty-five years for that promise to be fulfilled. Daniel served the Lord his God faithfully, but was thrown into the lion's den. Joseph was imprisoned for thirteen years for a crime he didn't commit. Jeremiah was cast into a pit because he brought the prophetic Word of God to Israel, and they didn't like it. Ezekiel was commanded by God to run naked for three years as part of his commission to rebuke Israel for her many sins, for the hardness of the people's hearts toward God, and for their rebellion against His Word. Hosea was commanded to marry a prostitute. Stephen was stoned to death for his faith. The Apostle Paul was shipwrecked several times, beaten horribly, imprisoned, and brought before the authorities to account for his behavior. There are numerous other examples of this kind of faithful suffering.

How then can individuals today preach and teach that all suffering is either a result of a lack of faith, or a result of sin?

Those who do are like Job's three friends who claimed that if he had more faith, or if he would simply repent, then God would heal and restore him. Eliphaz and his two friends were speaking a measure of truth. However, like many today, although they had the correct words, they did not have the correct application. Thus, their counsel was wrong. Unfortunately, large numbers of people in the Body of Christ have been hurt by individuals who have prophesied to, or counseled, those in the midst of suffering out of their own pet doctrine. While there may be a measure of biblical truth in what they say, ultimately they misuse and abuse the spiritual authority entrusted to them. Unlike Jesus, they do not truly seek the counsel of their Heavenly father. They do not judge as they hear, but rather with the sight of their eyes. (John 5:30)

If we as a Body truly desire to see the Glory of God, we must understand that "it is God which works in us both to will and to do of His good pleasure." (Philippians 2:13) Our God is a consuming fire. He is a holy fire, and He burns away all the dross in our lives. We cannot stand before Him with sin in our life. True, His blood covers us, but that does not mean that we can live a life of hidden sin and expect to stand in His Holy Presence. Nor can we expect our lives to be entirely free from the trials which are ordained, or allowed, by God. The Lord desires His bride to be a Body without spot or wrinkle. To that end, He chastises those whom He loves, and He refines all who seek to come into His Presence.

One sure sign that God is working in your life is that everything will begin to heat up.

As Bob Sorge points out in his book, **The Fire of Delayed Answers,** God is a Holy blacksmith who grabs hold of us with His mighty hands and thrusts us into His fiery furnace. When the fire gets hot enough, we become malleable. Then, He pulls us from the coals of testing, lays us upon the anvil of destiny, and begins to hammer us into the shape of things to come.

This is not a process that any of us relishes, or looks forward to. Yet, it is a necessary one if we are to become "vessels of honor" in His kingdom.

We are measured by how well we respond to what God is doing in our lives, not by how prosperous we are, how big our ministry is, or even how many people we are responsible for leading to salvation. When we grumble and complain about our circumstances, or mutter against those who have been given authority over us, we run the risk, like Miriam, of incurring God's displeasure.

Miriam was Moses' sister, but she wasn't happy with her brother because he married and Ethiopian woman. She and Aaron rebelled against Moses. They said, "Has the Lord indeed spoken only by Moses? Has He not also spoken by us?" (Numbers 1:3) In effect, they were saying that Moses was not the only one who heard clearly from God, and who was he to think that he should be God's only mouthpiece? Scripture tells us that God heard their murmuring and complaining, and that He appeared "suddenly" to all three of them. (v. 4)

That must have been quite a sight!

God told Miriam and Aaron in no uncertain terms that while He spoke to His prophets in dreams and visions, He chose to speak to Moses "face to face." He then asked them, "Why are you not afraid to speak against my servant Moses?" (v. 8b)

Beloved, we must be very careful how we talk about, and to, our God. We must be very careful how we respond to those whom God has placed in authority over us. We must also be careful not to ascribe to the enemy the work God is doing in our lives to refine us. He is not only jealous over His Name, but over His Word as well. He watches over it to perform it. (Jeremiah 1:12) It is He who commands so that we may obey, not vice versa. If we embrace what He is doing in, and through us, regardless of the circumstances, and if we don't waste our trials, He will bring us through the fire and refine us as silver and gold. As we cry out for His Glory, as we cry out for His Holy Fire, as we cry out for Him to manifest in unprecedented ways, we need to heed the words of Malachi:

But who can endure the day of His coming? And who can stand when He appears? For He is like refiner's fire and launder's soap. He will sit as a refiner and purifier of silver; He will purify the sons of Levi, and purge them as gold and silver, that they may offer to the Lord an offering in righteousness. (Malachi 3:2-3)

Job recognized the necessity of pressing through his trial in order to receive the blessings of God. It wasn't easy for him. He spent a measure of time crying out to God in frustration, because he knew he had not sinned and he wanted to know why he was suffering. Yet, in the end, he realized that when God was finished with him he would be as fine gold. (Job 23:10)

What exactly does this mean?

There are four key things that Job learned out of his ordeal.

God can do everything. God's purposes will not be frustrated, or prevented, by anything. Job also learned he had a limited understanding of God, because God's ways are higher than man's. Most importantly, Job learned that although he had heard and obeyed God in the past, he needed to come to the place where he had a more intimate relationship with Him. He needed to come to the place of *seeing* God. (Job 42:2-5)

As God refines us, He takes us through a similar process.

We learn in, and through, our suffering that nothing is impossible with God. Instead of His omnipotence being simply a tenet of our faith, we learn that what God begins He completes. We learn that He doesn't make mistakes. We also learn that all things work together for the good of those who love Him, even those things the enemy intends for evil. It takes time, but we eventually come to the place of trust Shadrach, Meshach, and Abednego had.

King Nebuchadnezzar was about to throw the three Hebrew captives into a fiery furnace, because they refused his command to bow down and worship other gods. He asked them if their God would deliver them. They replied, "If it be so, our God whom we serve is able to deliver us from the burning fiery furnace, and He will deliver us out of your hand, O king. But if not, be it known unto you, O king, that we will not serve your gods, nor worship the golden image which you have set up." (Daniel 3:17-18)

A powerful statement was being made here.

The three Hebrew men acknowledged that even though they knew God was *able* to deliver them, *He might choose not to*. They knew, and believed, that even if He chose not to deliver them from the fire, He would still deliver them from the king's authority to put them to death, because He is the greater authority. Finally, they made the point that regardless of whether or not God delivered them from the fiery furnace, they would not bow down and observe other gods.

Few of us have ever been asked to display this level of faith. Yet, many of us suffer in other ways–physically, emotionally, financially, and so on. How do we respond? Are we steadfast in our faith, or do we complain and murmur, comparing ourselves to others? Are we as certain as these three men that God will deliver us from the hand of the fowler? If we truly desire to "see" God, we must believe that "Many are the afflictions of the righteous, but the Lord delivers him out of them all." (Psalm 34:19)

Job also learned that God's purposes are never frustrated.

Often, God does not deliver us immediately from our trials. Rather, He sustains us through them, if we allow Him to do so. His delay is not His denial. We may well learn more by walking through the fire and emerging on the other side stronger and wiser than had we simply been plucked from the midst of them.

The classic biblical example of this is Joseph. At seventeen, Joseph had a series of visions. Because of youthful naiveté, and pride, he spoke the visions out, incurring the wrath of his brothers. He ended up being sold into slavery, accused of a heinous crime he did not commit, and thrown into prison for thirteen years. At the moment when it seemed that he would be delivered, his pride rose up yet again. Because of this, God allowed him to stay in prison for an additional two years to further refine him. Yet through it all we have no record that Joseph ever complained.

Ultimately, Joseph was appointed by Pharaoh as ruler over all of Egypt. Pharaoh also gave Joseph a new name: *Zaphnath-paaneah*. The Egyptian translation is "abundance of life." Jerome, the fourth century Christian biblical scholar who prepared the Latin version of the Bible, translated the name as "savior of the world." When we endure the trials God sets before us, and when we endure well, as both Job and Joseph did, we are truly walking in the abundance of God's Life. As a result, the world sees in us the true Savior of the world. This is the way that "Christ in us, the hope of glory," truly manifests to a lost and dying world. (Colossians 1:27)

God's Glory is the only hope fallen humanity has.

It is not simply meant to be something believers partake of self-ishly and revel in. God's Glory is the Light of the world. The unsaved mind cannot even begin to comprehend the plans and purposes of God. Even those of us who endeavor to walk with Him intimately struggle in this area. Nevertheless, God, in His infinite wisdom, has chosen to operate in, and through, His creation. What a radical concept. The Creator of the universe living inside of the creation! Yet, as Jesus tells us, new wine cannot be put into old wineskins because they will burst. (Matthew 9:17)

Unfortunately, many have been taught today that the mercy of God means instant deliverance from trials and tribulations. That is simply not true, as those who have endured extended tribulation will tell you. While it is true that He is not willing that any should perish, and that His mercies are new every morning, He does allow His saints to go through difficult times that He might build their character into His image and likeness.

During those times when God allows us to work out our salvation with fear and trembling, we would do well to remember that the Almighty has a purpose for each and every one of us, and that He will bring it to pass. (Ephesians 1:11)

One of the main things lacking in the Body of Christ today is a firm understanding of the sovereignty of God. This is the third lesson Job learned out of his trial.

We must come to accept that God does what He pleases, because it is He who created us, and not vice versa. The Jews have a firm grasp of this concept. And this is one of the main concepts that we need to learn from them. God Almighty, the Holy One of Israel, the Ancient of Days, the Creator of Heaven and Earth is the Great and Mighty King. None can stand before Him. None can compare to Him. He is the Ruler of the universe. We do not always need to understand why He allows things to happen to us.

God does not expect us to *understand* Him; He expects us to *obey* Him.

Job learned obedience by the things which he suffered. Thus, he was conformed into the image of Christ, even though Christ had not yet come in the flesh.

Hebrews 5:7-9 sets forth the process we go through in learning obedience, and the ensuing result. First, we cry out to God for help in our prayer life because we know, and believe, that He is able to deliver us. God hears our cry and reaches out to us with His Love. It is His Love that will sustain us and uplift us in our darkest moments.

By submitting to our trial, instead of resisting it, we are acknowledging that God is in control, and sovereign. We are trusting that He will not allow us to be tempted, in any shape or fashion, more than we can endure. In this, we demonstrate our reverent fear of Him. Our submission to His purposes, even when we don't like what is happening to us, is our acknowledgment that we accept Him as our Lord, as well as our Savior. God brings us through the trial, refining our character as silver and gold in the process. Through it all we are made complete in Him, because of our obedience.

God does not glory in our sacrifice.

It is our obedience that *releases* His Glory.

This brings us to the fourth, and most important, lesson Job learned.

Job's relationship to God prior to his trials is not specifically stated, but we can imagine that he must have had some level of revelation of His Heavenly Father, because God told Satan that there was none like him in the earth, that he was perfect and upright. The Hebrew words used in this passage for perfect and upright have the sense of *complete*, or *undefiled*, and *righteous*.

This is an extraordinary statement from God, because at the time of Job the Ten Commandments had not yet been given. Job was undefiled in the eyes of God, yet he had no law to go by. He was considered righteous, yet Christ had yet to come. Only one other man in Scripture met these qualifications, and that was Abraham. God said of him, "Abraham obeyed My Voice and guarded My commandments, My statutes, and My laws." (Genesis 26:5)

Here we have two men who knew the laws of God, guarded them, and kept them *before* God published them in the Earth! In Abraham's case, God rewarded him by multiplying his seed as the stars of heaven and blessing all the nations of the Earth through his offspring. (Genesis 26:4) As for Job, God not only restored all that the devil had taken, but blessed him abundantly above all he could ask or think. (Job 42:10)

Yet for all Job's favor with God, he was lacking something.

Job knew the voice of God, and he obeyed it. Yet, it seems clear from the context of the story that Job did not have the level of intimacy God desired of him. Job says, "I have heard You by the hearing of the ear, but now my eye sees You." (Job 42:5) For all his faithfulness and devotion, Job lacked a first-hand experience with God. His trials and tribulations forced him to reconsider all that he believed. He went from saying, "For the thing which I greatly feared is come upon me," (Job 4:25) to repenting that he had ever questioned God's goodness and mercy, and praying for those who tried to convince him that his suffering was a result of sin. (Job 42:1-10)

Many Christians still believe God punishes them with suffering, even when they haven't done anything wrong. Like Job, they harbor a hidden fear–no matter how blessed they seem to be, sooner or later God is going to judge them and find them lacking. Beloved, our sins have already been judged—at the Cross of Christ. We are not supposed to live in fear, but in freedom. Is it possible that Scripture teaches us that God already judged all our sin while He was hanging on that bloody Cross? That for believers there is no more judgment of sin until the Great White Throne judgment spoken of in the Book of Revelation?

While it is true God cannot, and does not, condone sin, it is also true that for those who have accepted Him for Who He is, sin no longer rules over us. Therefore, there is no need for ongoing judgment. The unrighteous suffer the judgment of Sin on a daily basis, not of God. Likewise, whenever a believer "falls into" sin, they, too, suffer the judgment of sin. This is why Paul can boldly say there is no condemnation to those who are in Christ Jesus. (Romans 8:1)

The root cause of our fear of God's judgment is our lack of understanding of our true identity.

An example of this is that many men find their identity in their work, and many women find their identity in being pleasing to men. In both instances, the things of this world are given more value than eternal things. We are told in Colossians 3:1-3: **"If you are then risen with Christ, seek those things which are above, where Christ sits on the right hand of God. Set your affection on things above, not on things on the earth. For you are dead, and your life is hid with Christ in God."** Whenever we place our faith in the things of this world, instead of in Christ, we make the Cross of none effect. We crucify again the Lord of Glory. This is not why Jesus came, walked among us, was crucified, and raised from the dead.

His desire is that we be like Job. No matter what happens to us, we remains steadfast in our faith in Him who is able to save us. More importantly, God's desire is that we become conformed to the likeness and image of His Son, Jesus. Being conformed to Jesus is a process. Maturity doesn't come instantly. The Apostle Paul calls it "working out our salvation with fear and trembling." "Whom shall He teach knowledge? And whom shall He make to understand doctrine? Those that are weaned from the milk, and drawn from the breasts. For precept must be upon precept, precept upon precept; line upon line, line upon line; here a little, there a little." (Isaiah 28:9-10)

Jesus calls us to be undefiled and righteous in the midst of a perverse and wicked world, to be like salt in the earth, and to shine as lights into the darkness. (Philippians 2:15)

We can only truly do this when we have a personal revelation of God that allows us to "see" Him as He is.

Prepare Him a Habitation

—∿—

Many today in the body of Christ yearn for a visitation from God.

Songs are written about the desire for His visitation; sermons are preached about it; and intercessors cry out for it from the depths of their hearts. What the songwriters, preachers, intercessors, and others who fervently cry out to Him all have in common is a burning desire to see God's Glory manifest in tangible and unprecedented ways.

That same fervent desire was initially birthed in the heart of a man called Moses.

God put that burning desire in Moses, and in every person who has ever earnestly sought His Presence, for a reason. Therefore, it is critical for all of us who cry out for His Manifest Presence—His Glory—to not only intellectually understand a simple, fundamental truth of His Word, but to allow it to become an engrafted part of us. This fundamental truth must become a living, breathing reality in the heart and soul of every individual who claims Christ as Lord and Savior before it ever will become a corporate reality in the Body as a whole.

God's desire has never been to merely *visit* his creation, it has always been His desire to *dwell*, or live with, His creation *on a permanent basis*. This is one of the reasons He speaks to Israel through the prophet Isaiah, and by extension to the whole world, saying of Messiah, "Therefore the Lord Himself shall give you a sign; Behold a virgin shall conceive and bear a son and shall call His name Immanuel." (Isaiah 7:14)

God *with* us.

God *in* us.

This desire of God's to dwell with, even inhabit, His creation is a simple truth, but one which all of us who seek His face struggle to grasp hold of and make a reality in our daily walk. Most come to the saving knowledge of Christ and never fully walk in the understanding that God has been seeking a habitation among men, His creation, from the beginning of Creation. Jesus was very likely alluding to this fact when He said, "The foxes have holes, and the birds of the air have nests, but the Son of Man has nowhere to lay His head." (Matthew 8:20)

Although God not only spoke to Abraham, Isaac, and Jacob, but visited them as well, it is in the patriarch Moses that we first see a man who both clearly articulates and experiences the manifest Presence of God—His Glory—in an unprecedented way. The story of Moses is a familiar one to many people, but a few key points are worth reiterating to make clear this point.

If we are to fully understand what God is saying to us in Scripture, among other things we must read the Bible in context. Part of that process is accomplished by filtering what is being said in the text through the mindset of the individuals He chose to write His Word down.

The Christian West refers to the first five books of the Bible as the Pentateuch, a Hellenized version of the Hebrew Torah. While Torah can, and does, mean Law, in its purest sense it simply means "teaching." It is commonly agreed that the author of the Torah is Moses. The Torah, or teaching, is composed of the books of Genesis, Exodus, Leviticus, Numbers, and Deuteronomy. It seems clear, at least in a general sense, these books correspond to teachings about Election, Redemption, Sanctification, Direction, and Instruction.

And it is in the Book of Exodus, a book that teaches us about redemption, or salvation, that we find something extraordinary.

Moses had his first encounter with the God of his ancestors while tending sheep on the mountain of God known as Horeb. Scripture tells us that he "turned aside" from what he was doing in order to more closely see the burning bush which was not consumed. The Bible then goes on to say, "And when the Lord (*Adonai*) saw that he turned aside to see, God (*Elohim*) called unto him out of the midst of the bush . . ." (Exodus 3:4)

Moses had to turn aside from the things that captured his attention and focus his attention on the burning bush before the Lord spoke to him. There are some who suggest that the burning bush had been there for the entire forty years, and that God was simply waiting for Moses to focus his attention on Him. This is an important principle for all those who genuinely desire to see the Glory of God manifest. We must turn away from those things which we think are important, and which consume our time and attention, and focus on the Lord of Glory. When we do that, He begins to speak to us in unprecedented ways.

Moses was forty when he left Egypt, and he spent forty years in Midian. While tending Jethro's sheep he certainly had a lot of time on his hands to think. Time to think about his life as Pharaoh's adopted son, about his true heritage as an Israelite, about the murder he committed in anger. Midian means strife, and Horeb means dryness, or desert. The Lord spoke to Moses once he'd left Midian, or strife, behind, even though he was in Horeb, a dry place.

This is an important truth.

The fundamental basis of redemption, or salvation, is forgiveness of—or better yet, atonement for—sin. It is sin which causes strife, or enmity, not only with our fellow man, but with God. It is sin that causes us to be estranged from God. And it is His forgiveness, accomplished by the shedding of His blood that reconciles us to Him. Without the shedding of blood, there is no atonement for sin. (Hebrews 9:22; Leviticus 17:11) Prior to the death of Christ, the atonement was accomplished by the blood of animals.

Yeshua HaMashiach, Jesus the Messiah, came as a better sacrifice, the *final* sacrifice for sin.

However, even though we are forgiven by the shed blood of Jesus, we may still find ourselves, from time to time, in a dry place. The exciting news is, it doesn't matter. Regardless of where we are in our walk, the Lord will speak to us as soon as we leave strife, or sin, behind. As soon as we turn aside from those things we are doing which are important to us and seek those things which are important to Him, He speaks to us loud and clear.

Beloved, we do not have to be in overt sin to be at enmity, or estranged, from God. We may simply have become enamored of the things of this world. Any time we put God *second* we are, in a sense, in strife or at enmity with Him. He is a jealous God and admonishes us in His First Commandment that we shall have no other gods before Him. (Exodus 20:3) His desire is that we keep our focus on Him, and Him alone. If we do that, He will guide our every step.

In many cases, once the Lord speaks to us, we, like Moses, often respond that we are inadequate to the call he has put on our life. The truth is, we *are* inadequate. But that doesn't matter either. Because He is *El Shaddai*, The All Sufficient One.

Yet, knowing God as *El Shaddai*, The All Sufficient One, is not enough. The Lord speaks to Moses and says, "I Am the Lord (*Adonai*): And I appeared unto Abraham, unto Isaac, and unto Jacob by the name of God (*El Shaddai*) but by My name *Yud-Heh-Vav-Heh (Adonai)* I was not known to them." (Exodus 6:2-3)

Something extraordinarily powerful is being said here.

Yud-Heh-Vav-Heh, YHWH, is known as the tetragrammaton, meaning simply a four letter writing. It is God's personal Name. In Hebrew tradition, it is a Name not to be taken lightly. The Third Commandment commands death for anyone who uses the Name of God as a curse. By the time of Jesus the only individual who used God's Name in any capacity was the high priest, and then only when he entered the Most Holy Place in the temple to make atonement for the sins of Israel on *Yom Kippur*, the Day of Atonement. In order to keep from mistakenly using God's Holy Name, the word *Adonai*, meaning Lord, was used whenever Torah was read. To this day, *Adonai* is substituted for The Most Holy Name in Torah readings all over the world.

In effect, God was saying to Moses, "Abraham, Isaac, and Jacob, your lineal ancestors, knew me as God Almighty, The All Sufficient One. But you, Moses, shall know me by My personal and intimate Name, Lord. Not only will I be your Savior, but I will be your Lord."

What an unprecedented commitment God was making to Moses!

God further promises Moses in Exodus 6:6-8 that He will do the following for Israel– deliver them (salvation), redeem them (resurrection), set them apart (sanctification), and take them for His people (identification).

Imagine the hope and expectation in Moses' heart.

Imagine his level of faith!

Nonetheless, Moses did not have an easy task. The Israelites' hearts had become hardened during four hundred years of bondage. Yet, in spite of their hardness of heart, God's word came to pass. He delivered His people from the bondage of Pharaoh, using the ten plagues and the miracle at the Red Sea. And what an awesome miracle that was. We read in Exodus15:31, "And Israel saw the great work which the Lord (*Adonai*) did upon the Egyptians: and the people feared the Lord, and believed the Lord, and his servant Moses."

Exodus 15:1-19 tells us that the people created a song on the spot and began to sing it to the Lord. The key verse for our discussion is: "The Lord (*Adonai*) is my strength and song, and He is become my salvation: He is my God and I will prepare Him a habitation (place of rest), my father's God and I will exalt Him."(v. 2)

Perhaps Moses, having just experienced the completeness of God's awesome deliverance, was speaking prophetically on two levels as he sang this song. Scripture tells us that first comes the natural, then spiritual. The first Adam was made a living soul, the last Adam a quickening Spirit. (1Corinthians 15:45-46) Could it be that Moses not only desired to build God an earthly habitation, but was crying out for Him to manifest His Glory in a unique and extraordinary way?

It is commonly agreed that Moses was expressing a heartfelt desire to prepare his Lord, *Adonai*, an earthly habitation. But perhaps he was also expressing prophetically what would occur in the fullness of time –the advent of *Mashiach*, Messiah, and the indwelling of the Holy Spirit.

Immanuel.

God with us.

God in us.

In Exodus 25:6, while Moses is on the mountain of God for forty days and nights, the Lord commands Moses to tell the people to build Him a "sanctuary" so that He may "dwell among them." He gives Moses specific instructions on how to build His "tabernacle." Moses does as he is commanded, and eventually the people work together to build The Tabernacle of Moses in the Wilderness.

Interestingly enough, it took nine months to complete the building of the Tabernacle, according to the pattern God showed Moses. The same length of time a human baby gestates in its mother's womb. When the Tabernacle was finished, we are told that "a cloud covered the tent of the congregation, and the Glory of the Lord (*Adonai*) filled the tabernacle." (Exodus 40:34). The Glory was so powerful, none could stand before it. When the Lord of Hosts shows up, every knee bows and every tongue confesses that He is Lord over all.

However, this dramatic manifestation of the Glory of *Adonai* was not enough for Moses. Even before the Tabernacle had been completed, he had a burning desire to see the Glory of his Lord and Deliverer. In Exodus 33:18 Moses cries out to the Lord saying, "I beseech you, show me Your Glory." God responds by telling Moses that he cannot see God's face, because no man can look upon the face of God and survive. However, God goes on to say, "Behold, there is a place by Me, and you shall stand upon a rock: and it shall come to pass, while my Glory passes by that I will put you in the cleft of the rock, and will cover you with my hand while I pass by: And I will take away my hand, and you shall see my back parts: but my face shall not be seen." (v.20-23)

Several points are worth examining.

First, this was not the Tabernacle in the wilderness.

The Tabernacle of Moses had not yet been constructed. This was a temporary tabernacle that Moses erected outside the camp and it was called the Tabernacle of the Congregation. (Exodus 33:7) Second, God tells Moses that he shall stand upon a rock. *Mashiach*, Messiah, Jesus is often referred to in Scripture as *The Rock*. Third, the temporary tabernacle would not have been constructed on top of a rock outcropping large enough to have a cliff. It would have been constructed on flat terrain, both for ease of construction and dismantling, as well as use. Fourth, there was no priesthood at this point in Israel's history. Although Moses is considered in type a priest, he was not one formally in the Levitical sense. Fifth, the translation is not literal, it is approximate, especially regarding the terms "back parts." We know that God, in His pre-incarnate existence, does not have a literal hand, although the imagery is used extensively throughout what is commonly referred to as the Old Testament.

I would like to suggest that something of far greater significance is happening here than first meets the eye.

Moses had a unique and unusual relationship with God. He was on intimate terms with the Holy One of Israel, the Ancient of Days, the Creator of Heaven and Earth. As we have seen, God revealed Himself to Moses as both *El Shaddai*, the All Sufficient One, and as *Adonai*, Lord. Additionally, Moses is the only man in scripture— prior to the arrival of Jesus—that spoke *"face to face"* with God. (Exodus 33:11) Moses found grace in God's sight, and God knew him by name. (Exodus 33:17) And, clearly, Moses had a burning desire to see God's Glory, His manifest Presence.

Scripture says that Moses was allowed to stand in a "place" by God. Where does God dwell? The prophet Isaiah wrote, "For thus says the high and lofty one that inhabits eternity, whose name is Holy: I dwell in the high and holy place, with him also that is of a contrite and humble spirit . . ." (Isaiah 57:15) Earlier, in Isaiah 26:21, he issued a prophetic warning: ". . . behold, the Lord comes out of His place to punish the inhabitants of the earth for their iniquity . . ."

What place is this?

Heaven. (1Kings8:30; Psalm 33:13-14)

We are also told that God would pass by Moses and reveal His "back parts" to the patriarch. According to the Harris, et. al. **Theological Wordbook of the Old Testament**, the Hebrew word for "back parts" can be translated in terms of time as opposed to a physical part of God's body. In this passage, translating the Hebrew in terms of time, instead of physical body parts, makes more sense, because there is no real suggestion that God has a physical body prior to the incarnation of Jesus. "Back parts" can easily mean "afterwards" or "later."

What am I saying?

It is entirely possible that Moses was literally taken out of time, into eternity, to stand in a place by God. And there, standing beside God, he had the cry of his heart answered.

He saw God's Glory.

What exactly did he see?

I believe Moses saw *Mashiach*, Messiah, Jesus, on the Mount of Transfiguration. The Apostle Paul writes, "For God, Who commanded the Light to shine out of the darkness, has shined in our hearts, to give the knowledge of the light of the Glory of God *in the face of Jesus Christ*. (2Corinthians 4:6) (Italics mine.)

The Gospels record that Moses was with Elijah on the Mount of Transfiguration. Both Moses and Elijah were prophets known for casting down idols and coming against idol worship. Moses dealt with the golden calf, and Elijah dealt with the prophets of Baal. Both Moses and Elijah were on intimate terms with the Lord, but Moses more so. Elijah was caught up to Heaven in a whirlwind and could very easily have been with Moses shortly after he was caught up to the Lord if Moses indeed stepped out of time into Eternity.

The Apostle Paul, in his epistle to the Church at Colossus writes, "When Christ, our life, shall appear, then shall you also appear with him in glory." (Colossians 3:4) And isn't it interesting that according to the Apostle John that the individuals who rise victorious over the beast of Revelation, who we know is Satan, over his image, his mark, and the number of his name "sing the song of Moses the servant of God, and of the Lamb . . ." (Revelation 15:2-3)

That song is the same one we discussed earlier.

The phrase "clefts of the rocks" appears in another interesting context—in the Song of Solomon. Also called the Song of Songs, this book unveils our Heavenly Bridegroom's search for His bride among the Daughters of Jerusalem. This story unfolds in two realms—the celestial, and the terrestrial. The earthly story is about a woman and her love for a man. But the heavenly story is about our Lord's pursuit of His bride to be. The Bridegroom is Jesus, and the bride consists of all those in the corporate Body who belong to Him. The Apostle John writes in Revelation 19:9: "Blessed are they which are called unto the marriage supper of the Lamb. And he said unto me, 'These are the true sayings of God.'"

We see a significant progression in the Song of Solomon.

In verse 1:4 the Shulamite woman says, "Draw me, we will run after thee: the king has brought me into His chambers: we will be glad and rejoice in thee, we will remember thy love more than wine: the upright love thee." First, she says, "Draw me." This clearly expresses her burning desire to see her lover, as well as her willingness to respond to him. Her request is representative of her intense spiritual hunger to be in the presence of God and comes as a result of her first meeting with her lover. Moses said, "Show me the way that I may know You and that I may find grace in Your sight. He also said, Let me see Your Glory. (Exodus 33:13,18)

Next, the Shulamite woman tells us that we will run after Him.

This is her commitment to her lover. If he draws her, she will run after him. We see a similar expression of commitment from the Apostle Peter. Just after the five thousand were fed, the disciples were on the sea of Galilee when the Lord approached them, walking on the water. The disciples cried out in fear when they saw Him, but He reassured them. Then Peter said, "Lord, if it is you, bid me come . . ." (Matthew 14:28) There were twelve disciples in that boat, but only Peter got out and walked on the water. I have often wondered what would have happened if the other eleven had joined Peter. Perhaps none of them would have sunk.

Next, we read that the king brings her into His chambers.

What does it mean to be brought into the chambers of Almighty God? Beloved, it means intimacy. Adam walked and talked with the Lord in the cool of the day. God revealed Himself in intimate ways to Abraham, Isaac, and Jacob. Moses spoke with Him face to face, and ultimately saw His Glory. If we truly desire to see God's Glory, we must be on intimate terms with Him. We must purpose to seek Him with all our heart, for when we do we shall find Him. (Jeremiah 29:13).

And where do we find Him?

In the cleft of the rock.

"O my dove, that art in the clefts of the rock, in the secret places of the stairs, let Me see your countenance, let Me hear your voice:

for sweet is your voice, and your countenance is comely." (Song of Solomon 1:14) The Lord desires communion with us and is ever beckoning us to Himself. As we learn to enter in to His Presence, we learn to turn aside from those things which distract us. In so doing, we find that we experience a progression expressed by the Shulamite woman. At first, she says, "My beloved is mine, and I am his." (v. 2:16) Then she says, "I am my beloved's, and my beloved is mine." (v. 6:3) Finally, she realizes that "I am my beloved's and his desire is toward me." (v. 7:10)

The pattern is clear.

God seeks us out, we run after Him, He draws us to Himself. And once we are in His presence, we rejoice in Him and remember His love. When we find Him Whom our soul loves, we hold Him and refuse to let Him go. (Song of Solomon 3:4b)

Abiding in Him

—〜—

W hy is it that so few Christians ever achieve an intimate relationship with the Lord? One reason is that few ever learn
how to abide with Him in the Secret Place of the Most High.

John Chapter 15 is the great abiding chapter in the Gospels. The
Greek word translated abide occurs seven times in this chapter. It
literally means to "dwell with a sense of expectancy."

When we dwell with the Lord in the Secret Place of the Most
High God, there is an expectancy that rises up within us. A holy
excitement is generated within our spirit that causes us to yearn for
God to manifest Himself.

We are told by Jesus that when we keep His commandments,
we demonstrate our love for Him. Because we love Him, we will be
loved by the Father, Who will manifest Himself to us. (John 14:21)
The word manifest in the Greek means to "visibly demonstrate."

What an extraordinary promise!

Imagine, the God who created the universe with the simple
command, "Let there be light!" tells us in His Holy Word that He
will visibly demonstrate Himself to us because we love His Son and
keep His commandments.

It doesn't get any simpler than that.

We know that we are able to love God because He first loved
us. His all consuming love is poured into our hearts by the Holy
Spirit. We have the unction to keep His commandments because
His perfect love flows in and through us. As our walk with the Lord

deepens, old things pass away and all things become new. This is the essence of becoming a new creation in Christ.

Why, then, is abiding such a difficult thing to do for so many believers? Perhaps the answer lies in the fact that few born-again believers truly understand the nature and character of the God of their salvation.

When God created man, He created him in His own image and likeness. Prior to the Fall, Adam and Eve were on intimate terms with the Father. They knew no fear, no disease, and no lack. Then, because of deception and disobedience, sin entered the world. Man became estranged from his Creator, losing not only his intimacy with the Father, but his immortal status as well.

Man became a slave to sin, and death entered the world.

Jesus came to reconcile us to the Father. He also came to destroy the works of the devil. The chief work, or power, of the devil is not sin, but death—not only physical death, but more importantly, spiritual death, which lasts for eternity. "For as much as the children are partakers of flesh and blood, He also Himself likewise took part of the same: that through death He might destroy him that had the power of death, that is, the devil; And deliver them, who through fear of death were all their lifetime subject to bondage." (Hebrews 2:14-15)

As we have seen in the chapter on Resurrection Power, when we embrace the concept that we are free from the law of sin and death because Jesus died and was raised again, and when we incorporate that truth into our lives on a daily basis, we overcome the world. But what does it mean to "overcome the world?" In order to answer that question we must look to the One who sets the standard, the Author and Finisher of our salvation.

In John 16 Jesus talks at length with His disciples about the third person of the Trinity, the Holy Spirit. He tells them that they will be persecuted, thrown out of synagogues, and even murdered in the name of God, because they profess Him as Messiah, the One True Son of God. But He also tells them not to be offended by these things, or to fear them, because when He leaves them another will come in His place, One who will teach and comfort them.

This dialogue is a mystery to the disciples. Jesus endeavors to speak plainly to them in order to reassure them. He tells His faithful followers that the Holy Spirit will "reprove the world of sin, and of righteousness, and of judgment. Of sin, because they believe not on Me, Of righteousness, because I go to my Father, and you see Me no more, Of judgment, because the prince of this world is judged." (John 16:1-11)

The Greek word "reprove" can mean to "convict" or "expose." The first portion of the passage tells us that the Holy Spirit will convict the world of sin by exposing *unbelief*. Jesus came in the flesh to redeem mankind from the curse of sin and death that entered the world through the transgression of Adam and Eve, but the world rejected Him. Failure to believe this is sin. We are told by the Apostle John that "He that believes on [Jesus] is not condemned; but he that believes not is condemned already, because he has not believed in the name of the only begotten Son of God." (John 3:18) Thus, the first step in overcoming the world is to believe that Jesus was who He said He was.

The prophesied Messiah.

Our Savior and Lord.

Next, Jesus tells His disciples that the Holy Spirit will convict the world of righteousness, because He will go to His Father in Heaven. The pure definition of righteousness is simply the character or quality of being right or just. It is sometimes associated with "equity," the characteristic of being fair and impartial. More specifically, righteousness is always associated with the character and nature of God. However, the only righteousness we possess, or partake of, is that righteousness imparted to us because the Holy Spirit lives in us. (2Corinthians 5:17-18; Romans 5:1-11; Philippians 1:9-11) Once we truly grasp this very important aspect of our faith, we can enter into the rest of God. This means we no longer strive to gain His approval through a works mentality. We are totally dependant on God for everything of value to us. This is what the prophet Isaiah meant when he wrote, "all our righteousness is as filthy rags ... But now, O Lord, You are our Father; we are the clay, and You our potter; and we are the work of Your hand." (Isaiah 64:6,8)

But why did Jesus say that the Holy Spirit would convict or expose the world of righteousness? He was clearly alluding to the fact of His resurrection.

In all of recorded history there has only been one individual who claimed to be the Son of God. As such, He walked among men as a man and never sinned, was crucified, and rose from the dead, victorious. That man was Jesus. In Acts 17:31 we read: "Because [God] has appointed a day in the which He will judge the world in righteousness by that Man whom He has ordained; *whereof He has given assurance to all men, in that He has raised Him from the dead.* (Italics mine)

The reproof for righteousness sake is clearly linked to the first reproof, which occurs because of unbelief. We are told that if we deny Jesus to men, He will deny us to His Father, God. (Matthew 10:33) This takes place at the Great White Throne judgment in Revelation 20:11-15. All whose names are not found in the Book of Life are cast into the Eternal Fire. Although this clearly seems to be a literal place of eternal torment, at the very least it means that the souls of men and women who deny that Jesus is the Son of God will spend an eternity separated from the One who created them in His image.

That, in itself, is a horrific thought.

Thus, the second aspect of overcoming the world is to believe in the resurrection. Many say that they believe in the resurrection, but few walk it out in their daily lives. As we saw in the chapter on Resurrection Power, living a life from the perspective of embracing the resurrection in all that we do results in a truly transformed life which in turn dramatically affects the world around us.

The third aspect of overcoming the world is found in the final portion of the above passage. The Holy Spirit will convict, or expose, the world of judgment by righteously judging the prince of the world–the devil himself. It is interesting to note that the Greek word used here for "judged" has the sense of undergoing the process of a legal trial *on an ongoing basis*. If we take this statement of Jesus literally, and there is no reason not to, what He is saying is that the Holy Spirit will take up residence in those who confess Him as Lord and Savior. Then, the Holy Spirit will, on an ongoing basis, *through us*, legally judge the prince of this world.

What this means is that we, the children of light, by being salt in the earth, actually judge the wickedness of the devil by our righteous behavior. The devil roams about, seeking whom he may devour, but the Lord raises up a standard to combat him. Jesus is that standard. And because Jesus is alive in us, through the power of the Holy Spirit, we can resist the devil, and he will flee.

Whenever we resist temptation, in any form, we judge the prince of this world.

This is the true victory of the Cross.

This is what it means to be set free from the law of sin and death. And this is why the Apostle John can boldly claim that, "Whosoever is born of God does not commit sin; for His seed remains in him; and he cannot sin, because he is born of God." (1John 3:9)

John is not suggesting here that we are sinless in the same sense that Jesus was sinless. The Greek word "commit" literally means "a continuous habit," or "to practice on an ongoing basis." What the Apostle whom Jesus loved is saying is that those who are born of God do not sin as a matter of habit on a continual basis. Rather, sin is something that they fall into as one entrapped by a snare. (James 1:2; Psalm 90:3; Psalm 119:110; Lamentations 3:46-47; 2Timothy 2:26.) The victory of the Cross is that whenever we do fall into sin, whenever were are snare or entrapped, God is faithful to cleanse us by His shed blood.

Jesus boldly tells the disciples, "These things I have spoken to you, that in Me you might have peace. In the world you shall have tribulation: but be of good cheer; I have overcome the world." (John 16:33) This is the fulfillment of God's word spoken to the serpent as a curse in Genesis 3:15 when the Lord pronounced His righteous judgment upon the one who had engineered the Fall of Man: "And I will put enmity between you and the woman, and between your seed and her seed; it shall bruise your head, and you shall bruise its heel."

Our real battle is not with flesh and blood but with spiritual forces under the control of the devil. When Jesus went to the Cross as an innocent man, as the Son of God, was crucified, and was resurrected, He ransomed back—for all eternity, and for all mankind—the keys of hell and death. (Revelation 1:18) The greatest punishment the prince of the world can hold over anyone's head is not physical death, as many suppose, but spiritual, eternal death. Once Jesus eliminated this threat, everything else the world, or the devil, threatens believers with pales to insignificance.

We should not be threatened by fame or by anonymity, by power or by weakness, by wealth or by poverty. This is why the prophet Isaiah said, "No weapon that is formed against you shall prosper; and every tongue that shall rise up against you in judgment you shall condemn. This is the heritage of the servants of the Lord, and their righteousness is of me, says the Lord." (Isaiah 54:17) When we are truly dead to the things of the world, we can say that we are dead in Christ and that we are raised with Him on a daily basis. This is what Paul meant when he told the Colossians that "your are dead and your life is hid with Christ in God." (Colossians 3:3)

We overcome the world because Jesus overcame the world. And because He went to the Cross so that the Holy Spirit could come and dwell within us. We overcome the world because His love is shed abroad in our hearts through the Holy Spirit. And because the shed blood of Jesus cleanses us from all unrighteousness. We overcome the world because Christ in us is the hope of glory. And because He promised us "Whatsoever you shall ask the Father in My name, He will give it to you." (John 16:23)

As we overcome the world, we are drawn into an ever-increasing intimacy with our Heavenly Father. As our intimacy grows deeper and deeper, we have a growing desire to abide with Him. In abiding, we are bathed in His Glory. And as we bathe in the Manifest Presence of God, His Glory, we can't help but reveal it to a lost and hurting world.

This should be our desire.

Seek intimacy with God, abide with Him, rest in His Glory, and then share it abundantly with the lost.

This was the heart of Jesus' message, evidenced by His last prayer prior to Gethsemane. "And the glory which You gave Me, I have given them; that they may be one, even as We are one: I in them, and You in Me, that they may be made perfect in One; and that the world may know that You have sent Me, and have loved them as You have loved Me." (John17:22-23)

The character of God is Love. Perfect love. His perfect love casts out all fear. It endures all things. It is not boastful. It is longsuffering. It doesn't seek self-promotion, nor does it puff up. Love does not rejoice in iniquity, but in the truth. Love bears all things, believes all things, and is ever hopeful. And it never fails. Regardless of how much faith we have, how much power, how many spiritual gifts, how much we suffer, or how many sacrifices we make, if we are without His love, we are nothing. (1Corinthians 13:1-8) We must truly understand and embrace God's character, not only as doctrine, but as personal experience as well if we are to abide with the Almighty.

There are many today in the Body who have large, visible ministries. They draw crowds whenever they preach or teach. They are wonderful storytellers. They make people laugh or cry with their words. They claim to have brought thousands, even tens of thousands to the Lord, and healed even more. They seem to have great authority with the Lord. But do they really walk in love? Do they really abide in the Secret Place of the Most High?

The test of abiding is found in John 15.

The only word used more in this chapter than abide is "fruit." And the message Jesus conveys to us here in this chapter is that He is the true vine, we are branches, and so long as we draw our life from Him we will bear much fruit.

But what kind of fruit is He speaking of?

Galatians 5:22 lists the fruit of the Spirit, and the first one is love. Proverbs eight is a discourse on wisdom, and verse nineteen tells us that the fruit of wisdom is better than fine gold. James 3:18 adds "But the wisdom that is from above is first pure, then peaceable, gentle and easy to be entreated, full of mercy and good fruits, without partiality, and without hypocrisy." Contrast this with the fruit of the soul spoken about in Revelation 18:14: "And the fruits that your soul lusted after are departed from you, and all things which were dainty and goodly are departed from you, and you shall find them no more at all."

Jesus is quite explicit in saying that not all who profess Him, even if they have prophesied in His name, cast out demons in His name, or have done wonderful works in His name, will enter the kingdom of heaven. He even goes so far to tell those whom He is rebuking to depart from Him, calling them "workers of iniquity." The key for Jesus is not being a well-known prophet, or having a world-wide deliverance or healing ministry, nor even doing mighty works in His name. Rather it is simply doing the will of God. (Matthew 7:21-23) Are all of these things the will of God? Of course. But it is the thoughts and intents and the motives of the heart that God looks upon in judging the quality of fruit, not simply the quantity of works.

Faith without works is dead. That is a fundamental of Scripture. We are called not only to hear the Word, but to do the Word. But we cannot escape the condition laid down by God when he called the Israelites to be a separate people unto Him, that through them He might demonstrate to the world His character. This condition, as well as the resulting benefits, also applies to those of us who have been engrafted in by the shed blood of Jesus:

> **If you walk in my statutes, and keep my commandments and do them . . .**
> **. . . I will have respect unto you, and make you fruitful, and multiply you, and establish my covenant with you.**
> **And I will set my tabernacle among you: and my soul shall not abhor you.**
> **And I will walk among you, and be your God, and you shall be my people. (Leviticus 26:3,9,11,12)**

When we fail to seek God for our every need and want, when we forget that it is only by abiding in Him that we have any authority or power, when we strike out on our own, believing He will honor what we are doing because we are claiming fruit in His name, we risk much. There is soulish, charismatic power that looks, tastes, and feels the same as God's anointing. We may operate in this soulish anointing for years, or even our entire Christian walk, thinking that the favor of God is upon us because of our soulish perception of what good fruit is.

However, if we are not drawing our sustenance from intimacy with our Heavenly Father, we will not manifest true fruit. We will not be longsuffering toward those who do not fit our sense of propriety, those who seem contentious to us, or those who hold to different doctrines. We will have a tendency to exalt ourselves in our speech and our actions rather than allowing God to raise us up in His time. We will invariably use giftings such as prophecy, the word of knowledge, the word of wisdom, and discerning of spirits to manipulate and control.

The danger in promoting our agenda and calling it God's is to become like Balaam. Balaam was a prophet who clearly heard from God and had His favor. But when Balaam sought the Lord on behalf of Balak, the King of Moab, and God told him what to do, Balaam continued to prevail upon the Lord because of his lust for riches, hoping God would change His mind. God knew the condition of Balaam's heart. Even though he was a prophet, anointed of God, he was deceived, because his desire for wealth had become his idol. And so God gave Balaam what he'd been asking for. But God's anger was kindled against Balaam, and He sent His angel to kill him. If God had not been merciful and allowed Balaam's donkey to speak, the angel of the Lord would have taken Balaam's life. (Numbers 22)

Understanding God's character also means having a reverential fear.

For the most part, the reverential fear of the Lord is not in the church today. If it were, we would be experiencing radically different congregational meetings, whether they are Sunday school meetings, Sunday services, praise and worship services, or conferences. Many in the Body cry out in genuine desire to see the Glory of God manifest in powerful ways, to see miraculous healings, to see the dead raised, to see nations come to repentance. These are all fruits of abiding in the Lord. But if we are truly abiding in the Lord, we will have a reverential fear of Him.

The Psalmist tells us that there is no lack or need with them that fear the Lord, that they keep their tongue from evil, their lips from speaking guile, they depart from evil and do good, and that they not only seek peace, they pursue it. (Psalm 34:9-14) How many of us today are truly evidencing the reverential fear of the Lord in our walk? Not as many as those who cry out for the fire of God to fall, for His Glory to manifest, for signs and wonders.

Perhaps if we really understood what we were asking for, we might not cry out so fervently. We might cry out more for His purging in our own lives, His chastisement of our souls, so that we might be set free from the very things that keep us from experiencing His awesome Presence.

David is an example of a man who did this.

Psalm 131:2 says, "Surely I have behaved and quieted myself, as a child that is weaned of his mother: my soul is even as a weaned child." This is an extraordinary statement from a man who was cursed by Shimei during his fight with Absalom over the kingdom and called a "bloody man" and a son of wickedness. One of David's closest men offered to cut off Shimei's head, but David responded that it was not Shimei who was really making the accusation, but God. (2Samuel 15:7-10) David was indeed a "bloody man," in the sense that he was a man of war, and because he had Uriah the Hittite's blood on his hand as a result of his adulterous affair with Bathsheba.

However, that is not how God saw him.

God saw David as a man after His own heart. (Acts 13:22)

True, David was a man of war, and he was far from perfect. But David's heart had always been toward the Lord. This is why God called Samuel to anoint him as king. It took years for God to prepare David for that position, and it took even longer for David to grow into the man God saw from the foundations of the world. But in the end, David is able to say that through it all he learned to "wean his soul" from the things of this world. Those of us who cry out for God's Glory would do well to follow his example.

How do we do this?

God created us to walk with Him as He walked with Adam in the garden in the cool of the day. Because of sin, however, we need redemption, so He sent His Son to live and walk among us as a man, to die for the sins of the world, and to be resurrected that we might partake of eternal life. Through the process of salvation He brings us to Himself so that we might experience Him intimately. It is the shed blood of Jesus that makes this reconciliation possible. Yet, many simply enjoy the manifestation of His Presence and Power only as long as it benefits them.

Many who desire to come into the presence of the Lord, like Ananias and Sapphira, are hiding secret sin because they have no fear of the Lord.

They may attend church regularly, praise and worship the loudest, fill their time doing good works, or give large sums of money. But that does not necessarily mean that they have a sincere desire to see God's Glory manifest. If these things are not done out of a right spirit, and are done as habit, or ritual, rather than out of obedience to the prompting of the Holy Spirit, our seeming faithfulness, our praise and worship, our good works, our generosity can all be idols.

Jesus addresses the issue of what happens when we place more importance upon the outward manifestation of our faithfulness rather than the inward.

He was in Jerusalem during Passover and He encountered a man who had been ill for thirty eight-years at the pool of Bethesda. He healed the man and incurred the wrath of the religious Jews because it was the Sabbath. The religious Jews were so incensed, not only did they persecute Him, they sought to kill Him. And not just because He had healed a man, but because He claimed that God was His Father.

Jesus answered their anger with a discussion about His relationship to God the Father, telling them He did not have a personal agenda. Rather, His desire was to do His Father's will. He then rebuked them for their behavior and attitudes and said, "Search the scriptures; for in them you think you have eternal life: and they are they which testify of Me. And you will not come to Me, that you might have life." (John 5:1-40)

Healing the man at the pool of Bethesda was a manifestation of God's Glory. Jesus walked in that Glory, not because He was God Incarnate, but because He was an obedient son. He was very specific in His discussion that He did not rely upon the testimony of men to validate who He was. He relied solely on His relationship to God, His Father. And it was God who bore witness of Him. First, by saying, "This is My beloved Son, in whom I am well pleased," and then by the works that Jesus did, because of that intimate relationship.

The religious Jews, on the other hand, claimed holiness based upon their adherence to the Law, not out of any fear of the Lord. If they truly had a fear of the Lord, and if they truly had revelation from studying the scriptures, they would have recognized Jesus for who He was. They would have embraced Him, instead of persecuting Him.

Dependence upon man to validate whatever it is you are doing is a sure sign that you are not abiding in the Lord.

We have seen that it is the lack of the fear of God that blinds us to the ability to see His Glory. And God's Glory, when it manifests, not only results in the miraculous, but it also reveals the darkest places of the human heart. We must all ask ourselves, "Do we seek God for what He can do for us, or for who He is? Do we simply enjoy the manifestation of God's Presence and Power, or do we truly desire to see His Glory?" If we seek Him for who He is, then we must seek Him with clean hands and a pure heart. Those who do will ascend the hill of the Lord and stand in His holy place. (Psalm 24:3)

We see in Israel, as a nation, and as a covenant people of the Lord, numerous examples of how the fear of the Lord, or the lack of it, affected their relationship with Him. God has always used His relationship with Israel to demonstrate to the world His character. The most obvious and striking example, of course, is the giving of the Law on Mount Sinai. Moses spent forty days and nights on the mountain, neither eating nor drinking anything, and when he came down, his face shined with the Glory of God. Yet the people could not look upon Moses' face because the Glory was so bright and they were fearful. They required him to put a veil on his face so that they could speak with him. And this caused God to lament over them. "O that there would be such a heart in them that they would fear Me, and keep My commandments always, that it might be well with them, and with their children, forever." (Deuteronomy 5:29)

The people did not have the fear of the Lord, rather they feared their sin being exposed and judged. Not Moses. He earnestly sought out the Lord with all his heart. In so doing he not only saw the Glory of God manifested, he walked in it and manifested it himself. The children of Israel wanted to see God's miracles. They weren't afraid of miracles because their sin could remain hidden. Moses wanted to see God's Glory. The children of Israel built a golden calf, all the while complaining that God had brought them out of Egypt only to let them die in the wilderness. Moses continued to beseech God to reveal Himself fully.

The irony is, God intended to reveal to all the Israelites not only His Law, but the fulfillment of His Law–*Yeshua HaMashiach*. Jesus, the Messiah. We read in 2 Corinthians 13-16:

> **... Moses put a veil over his face that the children of Israel could not steadfastly** *look to the end of that which is abolished*:
>
> **But their minds were blinded: for until this day remains the same veil untaken away in the reading of the old testament, which veil is done away in Christ.**
>
> **But even unto this day, when Moses is read, the veil is upon their heart.**
>
> **Nevertheless, when [the heart] shall turn to the Lord, the veil shall be taken away. (Italics mine.)**

Many who profess Christ as their Savior still have a veil upon their minds as well. They have not made Jesus their Lord, and thus do not have the reverential fear of the Lord. One who walks in the fear of the Lord will obey God, even if he or she has nothing to gain. It is easy to follow after the Lord when you believe there is a blessing in obeying, but what if there is no discernable benefit? Do you still pursue Him? We who seek His Glory must always ask ourselves whether we seek God, or the offices of God. Do we seek His face, or His hand? It is one thing to desire His power, and entirely another to desire only Him. Many who claim their hearts are for the Lord really only seek the recognition walking in His power and authority brings.

There are many today who seem to have great authority with men, yet they may well not have any authority with God. In contrast, there are many who seem to have no authority among men, perhaps they are even hidden, and yet they have great authority with God. Our desire should not be to be recognized and known among men for our great works, or our visible giftings. Rather we should seek the approbation of the One from whom all true authority stems. It is He who sets up and brings down the kings of the earth. Jesus commanded His disciples to "fear not them which kill the body, but are not able to kill the soul: but rather fear Him which is able to destroy both soul and body in hell." (Matthew 10:28)

But what is it that God desires?

What is His heart?

Perhaps a key can be found in the Books of Isaiah and Matthew.

"Thus says the Lord, The heaven is my throne and the earth is My footstool: Where is the house that you build Me? And where is My rest? The one I esteem is he who is humble and contrite in spirit, and trembles at My Word." (Isaiah 66:1-2) "And Jesus said unto him, The foxes have holes, and the birds of the air have nests; but the Son of Man has no place to lay His head." (Matthew 8:20)

God desires to abide in us. His resting place is in us. We are His temple, His true earthly habitation. He lives in us through the power of the Holy Spirit. When we yield ourselves to Him, He guides our every step. The Apostle Paul puts it this way:

Now therefore you are no more strangers and foreigners, but fellow citizens with the saints, and of the household of God;

And are built upon the foundation of the apostles and prophets, Jesus Christ himself being the chief corner stone;

In whom all the building fitly framed together grows unto a holy temple in the Lord;

In who you are also built together for a *habitation of God* through the Spirit. (Ephesians 2:19-22) (Italics mine)

When we have an intimate relationship with our Heavenly Father, He will increase, and we will decrease. As His Love increases in us, we will begin more and more to exhibit that love to others. According to Jesus the greatest example of love is laying down one's life for his friends. (John 15:13) Jesus went even further. He gave His life for the whole world. He not only set the example, but made it possible for us to lay down our lives for others. When Jesus asked Peter if he truly loved Him, and Peter responded three times that he did, Jesus replied, "Feed my sheep." (John 21:15-17) When we are truly abiding in Him, we will feed His sheep. And, even more exciting, we will love Jesus as much as the Father loves Jesus. (John17:26)

This then, is abiding.

To seek intimacy with the Father through the Son, to rest in His Presence with a sense of expectancy, to listen carefully to what the Father commands, and to obey Him without hesitation. In some ways, it is a daunting task. But the rewards far outweigh the cost.

We who sincerely cry out for the Glory of God, can, and must, rise to the challenge.

From Glory to Glory

—ᜦᜦ—

Approximately seven hundred and fifty years before the birth of Messiah, God spoke to His covenant people, Israel, through the prophet Isaiah. He warned them of His coming judgment if they continued to sin against Him, but He also spoke to them of His desire to bring them into complete restoration and reconciliation with Him. Isaiah tells God's people that if they want God to give them knowledge and teach them His ways, they must be "weaned from milk and drawn from the breast." (Isaiah 28:9) He further tells them that this is a process which builds upon itself, line upon line, precept upon precept.

This admonition to Israel is valid for us today.

If we truly want to see the Glory of God manifest in our lives, we also must allow God to wean us from milk and give us His meat. In other words, the redemptive nature of God operates progressively in our lives, ever drawing us deeper and deeper into Him. The author of Hebrews says it best:

> **For every one that uses milk is unskillful in the word of righteousness; for he is a babe.**
>
> **But strong meat belong to them that are of full age, even those who by reason of use have their senses exercised to discern both good and evil.**
>
> **Therefore, leaving the principles of the doctrines of Christ, let us go on unto perfection; not laying again the**

foundation of repentance from dead works, and of faith toward God,

Of the doctrine of baptisms, and of laying on of hands, and of resurrection from the dead, and of eternal judgment. (Hebrews 5:13-6:2)

This is an extraordinary passage. Much is being said here. However, we only have space and time to briefly touch upon some key points.

The progression in this passage is straightforward.

Milk is symbolic of several things in Scripture, one of which is the basic principles of salvation. (1Peter 2:2) The Apostle Paul writes to the Church at Corinth and tells them that although he desired to speak to them of deep, spiritual matters, he wasn't able to do so because they were behaving as if they were babes in Christ instead of those who had grown into maturity. They were still feeding on milk. Paul wanted to give them meat. He desired to speak to them, not about worldly wisdom, but about the wisdom of God. He chastised them, gently, telling them that the wisdom of God is a mystery to the world, or the unsaved, because the natural mind cannot comprehend the mysteries of God. He also told them that the mystery of the knowledge of God had been hidden from the foundations of the world, reserved for those who would earnestly seek Him. (1Corinthians 2:6-10)

Paul's point was that he could not speak freely to them of deep, spiritual matters because, even though they were professing Christ as Savior, they were still behaving carnally. They knew Jesus as Savior, but not as Lord. He went on to define carnal behavior as "envying, strife, and divisions." (1Corinthians 3:3)

This type of carnal, or worldly, behavior is typical of those who simply profess Christ as Savior, but have not allowed Him to become their Lord.

One who is envious desires to possess what another has. If an individual persists in that state of mind long enough, they begin to seek ways to take from others what they desire, which results in strife. Invariably, this leads to divisive behavior, which destroys. This is why Paul told the Corinthians that it doesn't matter who plants, or who waters, because it is only God who can bring forth the increase. (1Corinthians 3:7)

A diet consisting purely of milk might be a good thing for babes, but if that is all an adult lives on, the body begins to show signs of weakness and disease. Eventually, the body wastes away. If we apply this analogy to the Body of Christ, it is clear from these passages, and others, that a spiritual diet consisting solely of milk results in envy and strife, which then leads to division. We know that a house divided against itself cannot stand.

When we strive to possess what others have, whether it is authority, gifts, power, or recognition, we commit sin. Miriam and Aaron did this to Moses, with dramatic consequences. So did Korah, the Levite, who conspired with Dathan and Abiram against God's appointed leader. Korah was jealous of Moses and Aaron. He accused the brothers of usurping power he believed belonged to the Levitical priesthood alone. Korah was motivated by feelings of inferiority. He, and those who supported him, were angry because they had been assigned to the service of the Tabernacle. They wanted the power and authority God had bestowed upon Moses. Korah said, "You take too much upon you, seeing all the congregation are holy, every one of them, and the Lord in among them; wherefore then lift you up yourselves above the congregation of the Lord?" (Numbers 16:3)

Moses could have responded out of his flesh, in anger, but he didn't. Instead, he immediately fell upon his face before the Lord. He recognized that God was the true leader of Israel, the True Authority. He had been given leadership over people only because God had commanded him to assume that authority. In spite of Moses' humility, Korah and his followers persisted in their rebellion. Because they were ultimately rebelling against the authority of God, He destroyed them, their families, and all their possessions. (Numbers 16:32-33)

God went even further.

Once He had destroyed the two hundred and fifty rebellious people with Holy Fire, He commanded Moses to tell Eleazar to take the censers out of the burning fire and fashion them into a covering for the altar of sacrifice in the Tabernacle. Calling the rebels "sinners against their own souls," God wanted everyone to remember that

He is Sovereign, and that it was He who had ordained and set up the Levitical priesthood, not Moses, or any other man. (Numbers 16:36-40)

In the Book of Jude we are told that the type of behavior exhibited by Korah and his companions—which germinated from envy, was watered by jealousy, and grew into open rebellion— is associated with the same type of rebellion committed by both Cain and Balaam. (v.11) Cain was angry that God favored his brother's sacrifice over his, and so he committed the first murder in the Bible. Balaam was prideful of the gifting God had given him as a prophet and attempted to use that gift for financial gain by cursing the children of Israel for King Balak. Jude says that individuals who behave like this ". . . speak evil of those things which they know not; but what they know naturally, as brute beasts, in those things they corrupt themselves." (v.10)

Strong words indeed.

We must be careful that we refrain from coveting what others have, and especially that we do not rise up and rebel against those whom God has ordained to His service. We would also be wise not to demean those things which God has given to us for His service by comparing ourselves to others. (2Corinthians 10:12-13)

The author of Proverbs tells us that there are six things that the Lord hates–a proud look, a lying tongue, hands that shed innocent blood, a heart that devises wicked imaginations, feet that are swift in running to mischief, and a false witness who speaks lies. When we add the seventh, one who sows discord among the brethren, we are told that all of these things in concert become an abomination to the Lord. (Proverbs 6:16-19) The Hebrew word "abomination" has the connotation of being morally disgusting, loathsome, or detestable. This word is also associated with those who commit idolatry. Whenever we fall into envy we are committing idolatry. We are esteeming ourselves more highly than we ought to by making a subtle determination that others are less worthy than us to receive God's gifts. An attitude such as this presupposes that we know better than God who should receive his gifts or authority. This type of behavior not only displeases God, it grieves Him. (Ephesians 4:29-32)

Along with unbelief, idol worship is one of the primary reasons individuals become entrapped by envy and strife, and estranged from God. While Moses was on Mount Sinai, receiving the Torah from the Lord, the Israelites prevailed upon Aaron to do something about their plight in the wilderness, because they were impatient. Moses was gone for forty days and forty nights. The number forty is most often associated with probation, trial, and the chastisement of the Lord. (1Kings 19:8; Jonah 3:4; Matthew 4:2; Acts 1:2) The people God had so recently delivered from the hand of Pharaoh beseeched Aaron to create a new god they could worship; one they could see visibly.

How quickly they forgot their deliverance.

Aaron hearkened to the voice of the people instead of the command of God. He collected gold from the people and fashioned it into a golden calf and built an altar before it. When the work was finished, the people brought their sacrifices to the altar before the golden calf, then began to eat, and drink, and frolic. The further irony is that Aaron not only called the golden calf "*Elohim*," God, but also referred to the idol as "*Adonai*," Lord.

God knew what was going o. He admonished Moses to hasten down the mountain, saying, the people have "corrupted themselves." Had not Moses intervened, God was prepared to destroy all the people He had delivered out of Egypt and start over. (Exodus 32:1-17)

When Moses arrived in the camp and saw the dancing, singing, drunkenness, and nakedness of the people he was very angry. One can presume that there were other kinds of vile behavior going on as well. Moses' anger was a righteous anger. He carried within his breast the anger of God. We know this because he did not act rashly or foolishly. Instead, he commanded all those who were truly faithful to the Lord to stand with him. The priestly tribe, all the sons of Levi, stood with Moses. The patriarch then commanded the Levites to slay all those who evidenced their rebellion against the Lord by refusing to stand with him.

Scripture tells us that three thousand were slain that day. (Exodus 32:25-28)

This is the same number of people that were added to the Church on *Shavuot*, the day of Pentecost, at the conclusion of the Apostle Peter's famous speech. (Acts 2:41)

It is no coincidence that three thousand perished in the shadow of Mount Sinai, immediately after the giving of the Torah, and that three thousand were added to the Church on *Shavuot*. When God gave the Israelites Torah He was cutting a covenant with His chosen people, through His representative, Moses, on the day known in Jewish tradition as *Simchat Torah*, the giving of the Law. It is celebrated during *Succoth*, the Feast of Tabernacles. In many ways it was a marriage covenant. God, the Father, was the Bridegroom, and Israel was His bride. The Ten Commandments were the *ketuba*, or His marriage vows. He was saying to them, "I will be your God and you shall be my people, and if you follow My commandments, I will prosper you and make you a great nation." The cloud, often referred to as the *Shekinah*, His Manifest Presence, His Glory, was the *chuppa*, or covering. It was the seal of His Word, the sign of His approval.

Similarly, on *Shavuot*, Pentecost, the risen Lord, *Yeshua HaMashiach*, Jesus the Messiah, was again making covenant with His people, through His representative, the Apostle Peter. Peter spoke directly to the Jews gathered before him and called them into remembrance of the promises made to the nation of Israel throughout their history of the coming Messiah, their Deliverer. He clearly established that Jesus fulfilled, in every aspect, all of the biblical requirements, concluding his speech with, "Therefore let all the house of Israel know assuredly that God has made this same Jesus, whom you have crucified, both Lord and Christ." (Acts 2:37)

Peter was telling them in no uncertain terms that Jesus was both their Savior and their Lord, their Messiah, the Anointed One of Israel.

Three thousand immediately responded to the call of God.

The same number of people who perished at the giving of the Law.

Moses physically destroyed the golden calf, denouncing the people's idolatry, calling them into accountability with their lives. Scripture tells us that he burnt the calf in a hot fire, ground the golden idol into powder, cast the golden dust into the water, then he made the people drink it. It is interesting to note that whenever gold is ground to a fine powder and immersed in water it becomes what is known as "colloidal." Colloidal gold is reddish in color—almost the color of blood. What did Jesus tell His disciples? **"Except you eat the flesh of the Son of man, and drink His blood, you have no life in you. Whosoever eats My flesh, and drinks My blood, has eternal life; and I will raise him up at the last day ... He that eats My flesh, and drinks My blood, dwells in Me, and I in him"** (John 6:53-54, 56)

Once Moses had destroyed the golden idol, he told the people that he had to return to Mount Sinai so that he could make atonement for their sin. (Exodus 32:30)

A powerful, prophetic statement was being made on this momentous day in Israel's history.

It is acknowledged by most biblical scholars that Moses is a type and shadow of Christ. Moses had just been with God on Mount Sinai for forty days and forty nights. He had also spent forty years in Egypt as Pharaoh's adopted son, then forty years on the back side of the desert learning to be God's son. His intuitive act was more than just the behavior of a man whose anger was out of control.

By causing the people to drink the ruby colored "colloidal" gold he was making it clear not only that God was jealous of His Sovereignty as God and would not tolerate idol worship, but that it was only by His blood that sin could be atoned for. And it was only by the shedding of blood that man could be reconciled to God.

Jesus made a similar, public statement.

We noted in the chapter on **The Living Torah** that when God gave Moses the Ten Commandments on Mount Sinai the imagery in Scripture is that of a wedding ceremony. God was the Groom, Israel was the bride, and the seal of the wedding vows, the *ketuba*, was the Torah

In John 2:1-11 the Apostle John records for history the first miracle of Jesus. It is a familiar passage to all who have spent more than a few hours in the Bible.

There was a wedding at Cana. Significantly, the wedding was being held on the third day of the week—Tuesday. In Jewish tradition, anyone married on the third day of the week receives a double portion of blessings. To this day, in Israel, there are more weddings on the third day of the week than any other day.

The wedding reception was proceeding nicely until the wine ran out.

Mary, the mother of Jesus, told the servants to do whatever Jesus commanded them. John tells us that "there were six water pots of stone, after the manner of purifying of the Jews, containing two or three firkins each." (v. 6)

The reference is significant.

Typically, stone pots were used to hold water that had been purified by using the ashes of an unblemished red heifer mixed with cedar wood, hyssop, and scarlet. (Numbers 19:1-9) The priests used this "holy water" to purify themselves before and after sacrifices, or if they came into physical contact with a dead body. In essence, the water was purification for sin.

The fact that there were *six* firkins of water is also significant.

In Scripture, six is often associated with the number of man, because Adam was created on the sixth day. Six is also associated with human labor, while seven indicates the Sovereignty and rest of God. In Genesis twenty two the burnt offering is mentioned six times. The seventh is representative of the Divine Substitute God would provide in the form of Jesus. And we see from the account of Nehemiah rebuilding the wall at Jerusalem that whenever a work of God is begun there is opposition. There were six aspects in which Nehemiah was opposed. There was grief (Nehemiah 2:10), laughter and derision (Nehemiah 2:19), wrath and indignation and mocking (Nehemiah 4:1-4), fighting and open opposition (Nehemiah 4:7-8), false conference with the intent to murder (Nehemiah 6:1-2), and finally false friends (Nehemiah 6:10-14).

When the six stone water pots were brought before Jesus, He commanded the servants to fill them with water. This was unheard of. Jesus was doing the unthinkable. In today's terminology, He was commanding that ordinary—or tap—water be mixed with purified, holy water.

Finally, Jesus turned the water to wine.

The governor of Cana was at the wedding and complimented the bridegroom, because the best wine had been saved for last. This too was contrary to tradition. Normally, the best wine was consumed first. Only when the guests were too drunk to notice would the older, less expensive, less desirable wine be brought forth. John records that this was the beginning of the miracles that Jesus did, and that he "manifested forth His Glory, and His disciples believed on Him." (John 2:11)

In essence, this is what Jesus was proclaiming to the Jews by this miracle.

He took holy water, representing Israel, and mixed into it ordinary water, representing the heathen nations of the world, commonly referred to as Gentiles. Then, by turning the water to wine, He was making the following public statement: "I am the long-awaited, prophesied Messiah. I have come to reconcile My creation to My Father. First to the Jew, then to the Gentile. (Romans 1:16) By the shedding of My blood I will make all who choose by faith to believe on Me a new creation. There will no longer be Jew or Greek, bond nor free, male nor female. All will be made perfect and one in Me. (John 17:23) All who accept Me as Messiah will be called the seed of Abraham. All will be known by My Father as One New Man." (Galatians 3:28-29; Romans 11:11-36; Ephesians 2:12-22)

It is a biblical maxim that first comes the natural, then the spiritual. (1Corinthians 15:46) The blood covenant was first proclaimed to Israel at the time of the Exodus. (Exodus 12:7,13-14). It was then confirmed in the wedding *ketuba*, the Ten Commandments, on Mount Sinai and codified in the Book of Leviticus, along with the revelation that the shedding of blood is the only atonement for sin. (Leviticus 17:11) The shedding of blood under the first covenant, the covenant of Torah, was the natural covenant. (Hebrews 9:18-24)

When Jesus publicly proclaimed the blood covenant at the wedding in Cana He was making the statement that the spiritual covenant was about to manifest. This covenant, the better covenant, the one prophesied by both Jeremiah and Ezekiel was confirmed the day Jesus was crucified, and ratified on the day He rose from the dead, the firstborn of God's new creation. (Hebrews 10:1-19)

Because we are "grafted in," by the blood of Jesus, we too can partake of the promises God gave to Israel. This is clear from both Old and New Testament passages. (Exodus 12:19,48; Leviticus 19:34; Deuteronomy 26:11; Romans 11:17; Ephesians 2:11-13)

These may well be several of things that the writer of Hebrews had in mind when he wrote of being unskillful in the word of righteousness. As we grow from infancy, to young adult, to maturity in God, our diet needs to change accordingly. If we are truly seeking God's face, and not just His hand, we should gradually be weaned from milk and begin to crave a more substantial diet of meat.

Strong meat, in the Greek meaning *"steadfast nourishment,"* belongs to those who have learned to discern good and evil by reason of their continued use of the Word of God. Those who have been so weaned are called by the writer of Hebrews individuals who have reached "full age." Elsewhere in Scripture they are referred to as those who are "perfect in Christ."(Matthew 19:21; John17:23; Ephesians 4:13; James 1:4) This does not mean perfect in the sense that Christ was perfect, i.e. sinless, but rather mature, or complete, in Him.

What is extraordinary about the above passage in Hebrews is that the author not only admonishes his readers to strive for "perfection" in the sense of being complete in Christ, but says that the *milk* of God's Word consists of such basic things as repentance, faith, baptism, laying on of hands, and resurrection from the dead. If these are the *basics* of Christianity, what are the deep things?

One answer is found the Book of Hosea.

"And it shall be in that day, says that Lord, that you shall call me *Ishi*; and shall call Me no more *Baali* . . . And I will betroth you unto Me forever; yes I will betroth you unto Me in righteousness, and in judgment, and in loving-kindness, and in mercies. I will even betroth you unto me in faithfulness; and you shall know the Lord. "(Hosea 2:16,19-20) In Hebrew, *Ishi* means *"my husband,"* and *Baali* means *"my Lord."* What God is saying here, through his prophet, is that there will come a time when His chosen people, Israel, will once and for all acknowledge Him not only as their God, but they will be to Him as a bride is to a bridegroom.

We who have been grafted in because of the blood of Christ are able to partake of this promise as well. (Romans 11:24)

Imagery throughout Scripture presents a clear picture of the progression that unfolds in the lives of those who seek God, ultimately resulting in the kind of relationship Hosea was speaking about. But perhaps nowhere is it as vivid, or complete, as in Ezekiel 47.

In this chapter the prophet describes a river flowing outward from the Sanctuary of God during the millennial reign of Messiah. At first, the river is only to his ankles. Then, it rises to his loins. Finally, it becomes a river that he cannot ford. The water is deep enough for him to swim in. The Lord says to him at that point, "And it shall come to pass, that every thing that lives, which moves, wherever the rivers shall come, shall live." (Ezekiel 47:1-9)

This then, is the progression.

He loves us first, so that we might Love Him. Initially, He is the pursuer and we are the pursued. He beckons to us, deep calling to deep. We are lost in our sin, yet He still draws us to Himself, not willing that any should perish and that all would come to the saving knowledge of Messiah. Many are called, few respond. We accept Him as Savior, and He begins the process of redeeming our souls. We are instantly delivered from the power of death, but we must work out our salvation with fear and trembling. We are saved, not because of any inherent good in us, but because of His Grace. Thus, none of us can, or should, boast in our salvation.

As babes in Christ, we acknowledge Him as our Savior, knowing that He has delivered us out of the kingdom of darkness into the kingdom of His Light. Gradually, He draws us into ever deepening waters, and we are forced to rely upon Him, and Him alone. In the midst of the fiery furnace, in the midst of our trials and tribulations, in the midst of persecution for the Word's sake, we come to know Him not only as our Savior, but as our Lord. We become, as Paul did, His bond slave. We incline our ear to His Voice, seeking to hear Him in ways we only dreamed about, so that we may do only that which He has spoken to us.

As He increases in us, we decrease.

We move from being His servant to being His friend. We move from being a babe in Christ to being young men and women. Because we are His friend, He reveals His mysteries to us. He lights a fire in our heart, so that we might shine as lights in the darkness. When we see Him as He is, we become like the disciples on the Mount of Transfiguration. All we want to do is build tents and stay in His Presence, forever.

Yet, He prods us, ever so gently, to leave His Presence and commands us to be salt in the Earth. He commands us to love our neighbors as we love ourselves, to submit to those He has placed in authority over us, to feed His sheep. Because we are His friend, and because He has shed His love abroad in our hearts, we eagerly seek to do all that He commands.

We are like the Shulamite in the Song of Songs.

At first, we selfishly claim that "my beloved is mine, and I am his." (Song of Solomon 2:16) We think that we are in control and that He exists to give us all that we ask because we profess our faith in Him. That is the way of babes. They demand a great deal of care and attention. They love it when they are the focus of everyone's attention around them.

As we grow in our relationship with Him and learn more about our beloved, we cry out, "I am my beloved's, and my beloved is mine." (Song of Solomon 6:3) Gradually, we come to understand that the Love we so desperately desire has already been freely given. We learn how to accept, and to rest, in His unflinching and all-consuming Love. We discover that His perfect and unfailing Love begins to drive all fear from us. We are no longer motivated to do things because we seek His approval. Instead, we know that we already have His approval because that is His nature, and because of the Cross. We begin to understand, as did Job, ". . . far be it from God that He should do wickedness; and from the Almighty that He should commit iniquity. For the work of a man shall He render unto him, and cause every man to find according to his ways. Yes, surely God will not do wickedly, neither will the Almighty pervert judgment." (Job 34:10-12)

Finally, as we spend time with Him, as we hide in His presence, as we soak in His Glory, we gain the revelation that "I am my beloved's and His desire is toward me." (Song of Solomon 7:10) We have learned that God is not a respecter of persons. That His gifts and callings are without repentance. That what He begins, He completes. And that all His promises are "Yes" and "Amen." We leave behind childish things and grow into perfection. We become complete in Him.

Now we are ready to be His bride.

This has been His desire for us from the beginning.

We are like the five virgins who have their lamps trimmed with oil. The parable in Matthew twenty-five tells us that the kingdom of heaven is likened to ten virgins who were carrying lamps and went forth to meet the bridegroom. Five had their lamps trimmed and ready with oil, five did not. The five who did not are called "foolish," because when the cry went out at midnight, "Behold the bridegroom comes," they left in order to find more oil and missed the bridegroom. Although they returned later and knocked at the door, they were denied entrance. The Lord said, "I know you not." (Matthew 25:1-13)

Beloved, in order to see His Glory, in order to experience His Manifest Presence on an ongoing basis, in order to walk on a daily basis in the fullness of His Love, we must have our lamps filled with oil and trimmed. We must be ready for Him when He comes to us. If we truly desire to call Him husband, and not just Savior and Lord, we must seek Him with all our heart, and obey what He commands.

We have seen in earlier chapters that it is the unregenerate areas of our souls that keep us from experiencing the fullness of Christ. Our spirits are willing, but our flesh is weak. The soul which is not weaned from the things of this world can be likened to the professing Church. Those who simply "profess" Christ love Jesus, but are not consistently obedient. They are like the Israelites who loved God, but disobeyed Him. They believe in the goodness of God, but not His severity. Like the children of Israel in the wilderness, their minds are darkened. When they encounter the Glory, they want it covered, because they fear their sin being exposed. Yet those who embrace the Glory know that "where the spirit of the Lord is there is liberty," and that "we all, with open face beholding as in a glass the Glory of the Lord are changed into the same image from glory to glory, even as by the Spirit of the Lord. (2Corinthians 3:17-18)

This should be our goal.

To behold His glory, so that we might be changed.

To do as the Apostle Paul instructed Timothy: follow after righteousness, godliness, faith, love, patience, and meekness. "To fight the good fight of faith and lay hold of eternal life."(1Timothy 6:11-12)

This is how we are changed.

This is how we behold His Glory.

His Precious Blood

—ɯ—

O ne of the most misunderstood and least taught about doctrines of the Bible is the blood of Jesus. It is also one of the most important fundamental truths of the Bible the devil hates without measure. Because of the power in the shed blood of Jesus, the enemy will stop at nothing to obscure, diminish, and ridicule its significance. Without the essential doctrine of the importance of the shed blood of Jesus, there can be no doctrine of the resurrection, and without resurrection there would be no Christianity.

In order to grasp the full significance of the blood of Jesus, we must start at the Creation, because it is in the Creation that God established all the fundamental precepts of the work of His hands.

God created man on the sixth day of Creation, along with all the animals in both the land and sea. Genesis 1:26 tells us that man was created in the image and likeness of God, and Genesis 2:7 says: **And the Lord God formed man of the dust of the ground, and breathed into his nostrils the breath of life; and man became a living soul.** In order for us to fully grasp what is being said in this particular passage of Scripture it will be helpful to use an expanded, more literal, translation of the Hebrew. **And *Adonai Elohim* fashioned Adam, as a potter working with clay, out of the minute particles of the Creation, and intensely blew into his nostrils the living breath of lives; and Adam became a living soul.**

We know from Scripture that Jesus created and formed the universe, and that it was He who did the literal work of creation.

(Colossians 1:15-18; Ephesians3:9; John1:3) Thus, it was He, *Adonai Elohim*, the Lord God, who formed Adam.

According to the **Theological Wordbook of the Old Testament**, the etymology of the Hebrew word *'adam* cannot be explained with certainty. Typically, scholars relate the word to the supposed original ruddiness of man's complexion. The word comes from the same root as the word for blood, which in the Hebrew is "*dam.*" There are at least four other Hebrew words used for man, with varying shades of meaning, but *'adam* is the only one used in the context of God creating man in His likeness and image.

This is very important.

Adam is not primarily a proper name, although it can be used as such. Perhaps the word Adam, in the context of the Creation, is in reality a combination of two ideas. God is often referred to in Hebrew in terms of the first and last letters of the Hebrew alphabet, the *aleph* and *bet*. In the Greek, He is the *alpha* and the *omega*, the beginning and the end. If we combine the idea of God represented by the *aleph* with the Hebrew word for blood, "*dam*," a more literal translation of Adam might well be "God's blood."

There are three Hebrew verbs used in the creation story–created, made, and formed. While they have overlapping similarities, there are distinct differences. The verb "formed" does not occur until Genesis 2:7, relative to the creation of man, and it is the participial tense. This participial verb tense is clearly expressed in Isaiah 64:8, "But now, O Lord, You are our Father; we are the clay, and You our potter; and we are all the work of your hand."

The Hebrew word translated "dust" has varying shades of meaning as well. It can, and does mean dust, particularly in the sense of minute particles. And the Hebrew word for "ground" or "earth" is most often associated with the red arable soil. But it can also mean the substance of Creation.

Putting all the imagery together, we have the Master Potter forming, or fashioning, a living being out of the very minute particles of the Creation, and then imparting life with an intense blowing in of His breath.

In Hebrew, the word translated "life" is actually plural, meaning "lives." The Hebrew suggests that what God was literally doing was imparting His Precious Blood into Adam while at the same time animating him with a spirit and a soul.

Thus, the breath of "lives."

In Leviticus 17:11 we are told that "the life of the flesh is in the blood." Certainly, when God formed Adam, He gave him blood. At the very least it seems highly probable that the name associated with mankind would represent the very life-force which animated him.

God's blood.

Now, let's look at the tripartite creation of man.

Mankind is a spirit being, who has a soul and a fleshly body. This tripartite aspect of man is certainly in keeping with the "image and likeness" of God the Father, God the Son, God the Holy Spirit. In his Epistle to the Thessalonians the Apostle Paul writes, "And the very God of peace sanctify you wholly; and I pray God your whole spirit, soul, and body be preserved blameless until the coming of our Lord Jesus Christ." (1Thessalonians 5:23)

We know from Scripture that salvation is progressive.

The first thing that is dealt with by the new creation is spiritual death. This is instant. When we confess Christ according to Romans 10:9-10, we are immediately translated from the kingdom of darkness into the kingdom of light. We are spiritually raised from among the living dead and given the Spirit of Life in Christ Jesus. (Ephesians 2)

Then, the process of working out our salvation with fear and trembling begins. This is the process of having our minds renewed and transformed. It is also the process of weaning the soul from the things of this world and bringing it into submission to the spirit. This is not an easy process, but God is faithful to help us overcome the world. Jesus went to the Garden of Gethsemane and wrestled with His soul, as a man, for three hours, bringing His soul into submission to the will of God so that we might be able to do the same. This is why Apostle Peter writes that the completion of our faith is the saving of our souls. (1Peter 1:9)

Finally, in the twinkling of an eye we will all be raised incorruptible and be changed in an instant. We will receive a glorified body. (1Corinthians 15:51-54) The same kind of body that Jesus had, after His resurrection. This is what the Apostle Paul was talking about when he said there is a natural body and there is a spiritual body. (1Corinthians 15:44) In all likelihood, we will look much like Adam and Eve looked before the Fall. The Glory of God will be our covering, and thus there will be no need for clothing. (Colossians 3:4)

Let's look at this concept of a "spiritual body" versus a "natural body" for a moment.

Scripture tells us that God made man in His image and likeness. We know that God is Light and in Him there is no darkness at all. (1John1:5) Light was the very first thing God created. (Genesis.1:3) Jesus is the True Light. (Revelation 21:23) The Glory of God is called the Light "which no man can approach, which no man can see." (1Timothy 6:16)

The spirit realm, then, is the realm of Light.

It seems highly likely that when God created Adam (God's blood) He created him as a being of *light* in some sense. We know that Adam had an incorruptible body until the Fall. It was not until Adam and Eve ate of the tree of The Knowledge of Good and Evil that mankind became corruptible flesh in the sense that he is today.

When Adam (God's blood) ate of the tree of the knowledge of good and evil, God's blood (Adam) became contaminated with sin.

God had previously warned Adam, saying "But of the Tree of the Knowledge of Good and Evil you shall not eat of it: for in the day you eat of it you shall surely die." (Genesis 2:7) Yet, Adam and Eve did not instantly drop dead when they ate of the tree of the knowledge of good and evil. A more literal translation of the Hebrew would be, "in the day you eat of it, in dying you will die."

God was warning Adam and Eve that just as He had given them the breath of "lives," His blood and His spirit, they would die twice if they ate of the one tree in the garden He had commanded them not to partake of.

First, and immediately, they would die spiritually, because they would no longer have access to His Eternal Life, the Tree of Life. They would lose the covering of His Glory. Eventually, they would die physically, because sin was at work in their bodies, which were no longer immortal bodies cocooned by the Light of His Glory, but mere mortal bodies of flesh and bone.

We know that first comes the natural, then the spiritual.

God gave Adam and Eve "coats of skin" (Genesis 3:21), dealing with the natural issue first. Man's body was now "corruptible," subject to death. Then God banished them from the Garden (Genesis 3:22-24), thus dealing with the spiritual issue. Because Adam and Eve no longer abided in the Presence of God, the Spirit of Eternal Life that covered them—God's Glory–was now replaced with the spirit of death.

In Hebrew, the word for "light" and "skin" is the same.

It is the Hebrew word, *"or."*

The only difference between the two is the use of a consonant for pronunciation. The letter *aleph*, the first letter of the Hebrew alphabet, is used for light, while the letter *ayin* is used for skin. An apparent word play in the text of Genesis 3:21 suggests the idea that man was originally created with "garments of light," and when he sinned he received "garments of skin." Several sources, including a number of *midrashim*, which are early Jewish commentaries on Biblical text, Philo, the Zohar, and at least one well-known Jewish scholar all identify the "coats of skin" in this passage as the physical, or earthly body of man.

Man was created in the image and likeness of God. God's blood flowed in his "veins." He lived in the Garden of Eden and ate freely from the Tree of Life. God's Glory was his "covering." Man disobeyed and ate of the Tree of the Knowledge of Good and Evil. God's blood became contaminated with sin. Death not only flowed in the blood, but had legal authority over the spirit of man. The Glory departed.

There are at least two interesting scriptures in the Book of Job that shed light on this perspective of the Fall.

First, when the devil appears before God—along with the sons of God, the angels—God asks him if he has given any thought about His faithful servant, Job. God then makes the point that Job was perfect and upright, that he feared God, and that he ran from evil. He also points out that Job maintained his integrity even though the devil had unjustly come against him, attempting to make him curse God and die. In essence, God tells the devil that Job was a righteous man. The devil immediately replies, "Skin for skin, yes all that a man has will he give for his life." (Job 2:1-6) The Hebrew word translated "life" is actually the word "soul."

The text seems to indicate that the devil was mocking God with his statement. His desire had always been to be like The Most High God. (Isaiah 14:12-15). That is why he rebelled and was cast out of Heaven. Perhaps what the devil was saying to the Almighty was, "You may have created man in your image and likeness, but I caused him to fall. Look at your magnificent being of incorruptible light now. He is nothing more than corruptible flesh and blood. I was the one who convinced him to disobey You by prevailing upon his pride. Therefore, I am the one who really is the most powerful."

Later, Job is talking with his friend Bildad, the Shuhite, about the calamity that has befallen him. In despair, Job expresses his loss of hope. Bildad responds with a discourse about what happens to wicked men, specifically those who do not know God. He says that destruction awaits by their side anxiously, ready to pounce on those who disobey Him. He then adds that destruction "shall devour the strength of his skin: even the firstborn of death shall devour his strength." (Job 18:12-13)

There are numerous Hebrew words translated "strength." In this particular scripture, however, the word translated "strength" literally means "separation." This is the only passage in all of Scripture in which this word is so used. It doesn't appear anywhere else. Additionally, the phrase "firstborn of death" literally means "the one who has the birthright of death." The literal wording in Hebrew is the following: "Calamity and destruction eats, or consumes, the separation or covering of his skin. The one who has the birthright of death shall eat, or consume, the separation or covering."

Because of man's disobedience, God's Glory, His Eternal Life, was replaced by the spirit of death. The imagery of this passage is that death consumes the covering of man. In the allegorical sense, the Glory is taken away. In the literal sense, the flesh of man fades away as the grass. (1Corinthians 15:39-44)

Sin separated man from God, and His Glory.

The skin is a reminder of that separation from the covering, or Glory of God. The high priest of death, the firstborn of death, the one who holds the birthright of death, is the devil. In Hebrew tradition, the firstborn male of the family is the priest of the family. He is entitled to receive the full inheritance of his father. Allegorically, Satan is the firstborn of death, just as Jesus is the firstborn of the new creation. Therefore, the devil's birthright was the power of death, just as the birthright of Christ is the power of Eternal Life.

The devil was reminding God of this fact by his statement.

There also seems to be confirmation of this idea in the burnt offering Israel was to give to God. The Hebrew word translated "burnt offering" literally means "ascending as smoke." This offering was called the burnt offering, because it was to be consumed completely, and the smoke would then rise to Heaven as a sweet-smelling savor to the Lord. (Leviticus 6:8-13) The burnt offering, unlike the sin and trespass offerings, symbolized the entire surrender to God of the individual, or the congregation. It also symbolized renewal and sanctification, a consecration to living the kind of life that would be pleasing God. The burnt offering had nothing to do with atonement or forgiveness for sin, as did the sin and trespass offerings. Rather, it was an acknowledgment of God's grace in the individual's life. Even the strangers who dwelled among the Israelites were permitted to offer burnt offerings to God so long as they had not committed any notorious offense.

According to the command of God, anyone who desired to bring a burnt offering to the Lord was to select an unblemished male from among the herd of cattle. The bullock was then sacrificed, and the priests sprinkled the blood upon the altar at the door of the Tabernacle. Then the bullock was to be flayed. Everything *but the skin* was to be consumed by the fire. (Leviticus 1:1-6) Because the skin is a reminder of man's separation from God it was not to be offered in this "grace offering."

Interestingly, when the sin or trespass offering was made the bullock was *not* flayed. Everything, *including the skin*, was consumed by the fire. However, only the priests were entitled to eat the skin. (Leviticus 6:24-7:8) In these offerings, the atonement offerings, the skin is consumed along with the rest of the animal because it is the reminder of the sin of man.

The key to understanding all of this is the blood.

We know that Mary, the mother of Jesus, conceived by the Holy Spirit. This is commonly called the Virgin Birth. A better term is Immaculate Conception, because God, through the power of the Holy Spirit, was the Father of Jesus. We know that a developing baby's blood never mixes with the mother's because of the placental function. Although the mother provides all the nutrients necessary to sustain life, the blood is manufactured by the fetus itself.

Thus, a baby can, and often does, have a different blood type than its mother.

This means that Jesus, when He was conceived by His Heavenly Father, carried His Father's blood. The same blood Adam carried before the fall. This is one reason Jesus is called the last Adam. "The first man Adam was made a living soul; the last Adam was made a quickening spirit." (1Corinthians 15:45) The first Adam and the last Adam had the same Father, and thus the same blood type.

God's blood.

The significant difference is that the first Adam ate of the Tree of the Knowledge of Good and Evil and sin entered the world, while the last Adam, Jesus, remained sin-free so that He might be the final sacrifice, the atonement for all of mankind's sin. (Romans 5:12-21)

Perhaps sin actually corrupted the blood in some fashion we have yet to learn about. One might even go so far as to suggest it was a kind of spiritual AIDS. The acronym AIDS stands for Acquired Immunity Deficiency Syndrome. In laymen's terms, the virus that causes AIDS ravages the immune system to the point that it cannot fight off disease. Although we often read that individuals die of AIDS, that is not exactly what occurs. In reality, individuals die of diseases which the immune system typically fights. Because individuals have the HIV virus, their immune systems are compromised to the point that they cannot fend off disease. This virus literally turns the body against itself.

Perhaps this is why the Bible says that the "wages of sin is death; but the gift of God is eternal life through Jesus Christ our Lord." (Romans 6:23) A more literal translation would be "the wages of sin are separation from God and one who is separated from God will spend eternity in outer darkness and will be in a state of eternal death; but the divine deliverance of God is the indwelling Life of God."

The last Adam, Jesus, had pure, undefiled, sinless blood. His blood never mixed with His mother, Mary. Yet, because he was born of a woman He was both God and man. This is what made it possible for Him to shed His blood to atone, and redeem, all of humanity from the curse that entered the world because of the sin of Adam and Eve. (Romans 5:12; Hebrews 9:12)

Jesus was the unblemished sacrifice.

He was, and is, the universal antidote for sin.

There is an interesting parallel to the creation story in Greek mythology that is worth examining at this point in the light of our discussion of the blood and salvation.

Prometheus was a Titan who stole fire from heaven, in defiance of Zeus, and gave it to mankind. Fire represents light and knowledge. The art of making fire was knowledge that the gods possessed and did not want mankind to have because they didn't want man to have as much knowledge as they did, and thus become too independent. As his punishment, Zeus sentenced Prometheus to be chained to a rock where by day a giant eagle came and sat upon his chest and devoured his liver. By night, his liver regenerated. Thus, he was condemned by Zeus to an eternity of torment. It is interesting to note that one of the chief functions of the liver is the purifying of blood.

Fortunately for Prometheus, Hercules rescued him.

What is extremely fascinating about this Greek myth is it's similarity to what happened to Adam and Eve as a result of the Fall. God commanded Adam that he could freely eat of any tree in the Garden of Eden, except the tree of the knowledge of good and evil. Presumably Adam communicated this mandate to his wife, Eve, because when she encountered the serpent she repeated the admonition against eating from the tree, but added something God never said. She told the serpent, not only were they to abstain from eating of the tree, but they were not to touch it as well. This misrepresentation of God's Word opened the door for the serpent to proclaim, "You will not die: For God knows that in the day you eat thereof your eyes shall be opened, and you shall be as gods, knowing good and evil." (Genesis 3:1-5)

Part of Adam and Eve's punishment was banishment from the Garden of Eden. The reason God did this was because He didn't want them eating from the Tree of Life. Why? Imagine this scenario. Eating of the Tree of Life is a metaphor for deriving sustenance from the very essence and nature of God—His Glory. By partaking of God's Glory on a daily basis, Adam and Eve were assured of Eternal Life. They were immortal. That was God's intent in creating them in His image and likeness. He intended to fellowship with His creation for eternity. He intended that His Glory would sustain them forever. To that end He created them to live in, and by, His Glory.

When they ate of the Tree of the Knowledge of Good and Evil, sin entered the world. God's blood became corrupted. Death reigned supreme. Because death was now at work in their bodies, if they continued to eat of the Tree of Life they would live in an eternity of torment. The law of sin and death would destroy their bodies on a daily basis, yet the Glory of God would constantly regenerate them. This is why God banished man from the Garden of Eden and set cherubim with flaming swords to make certain they did not partake of the Tree of Life. (Genesis 3:22-24)

In both the Old and New Testaments it is clear that God does not take any pleasure in seeing His creation, mankind, suffer the consequences of sin.

In Ezekiel eighteen there is a discourse about sin and righteousness. God specifically speaks through His prophet to tell His chosen people that if one who is righteous under the law turns from his righteous behavior and commits iniquity, his soul will die in the same manner as one who is wicked. But if the wicked man turns from his sinful ways and does what is lawful and just, his soul shall live. He concludes by saying, "Cast away from you all your transgressions whereby you have transgressed and make you a new heart and a new spirit: for why will you die, O house of Israel. For I have no pleasure in the death of him that dies, says the Lord God: wherefore turn yourselves and live." (Ezekiel 18:32)

The Apostle Peter reiterates this Word of the Lord, reminding the Jews that God is longsuffering and not willing that any should die in sin, but that all would repent and gain eternal life. He also tells them that all who call upon the Name of the Lord shall be saved. (2Peter 3:9; Acts 2:21)

We have seen that the key to the salvation both Ezekiel and Peter were referring to is believing that Jesus is the Son of God, that He came and walked as a man, that He was crucified, then raised from the dead. All of this happened because the blood became contaminated by sin. But Jesus came with His Precious Blood to atone for sin once and for all. (1Peter 1:18-25)

Not only did Jesus shed His blood for us, but He shed it for Himself that He might be raised from the dead. (Hebrews 9:12, 13:20) His blood is the key that unlocks the mystery of salvation. The blood sacrifices to God, prior to the sacrifice of Jesus, were necessary so that the patterns of the Heavenly things could be purified. (Hebrews 9:23) But in order for the Heavenly things to be purified, Jesus had to die and shed His sinless blood. (Hebrews 10:1-10) Perhaps this is why Jesus admonished Mary not touch, or cling, to Him because He had not yet ascended to His Father in Heaven (John. 20:17); because He had not yet carried His blood to the Mercy Seat in Heaven.

In the Gospel of John, immediately after Jesus fed the five thousand, He engaged those who sought to follow Him in an unusual discussion. They asked Him what they had to do so that they too could work the works of God. He replied, "This is the work of God, that you believe on Him whom He has sent." (John 6:29) The Jews pressed Him further, asking for a sign. He told them that "I am the bread of life and that those who eat of Me will never hunger or thirst." He informed them that all who see the Son and believe will have everlasting life because of the resurrection. (John 6:35, 39-40)

This discourse did not set well with many of the Jews.

They murmured among themselves because Jesus claimed to be the bread of life from Heaven, thus equating Himself with God the Father. Finally, Jesus told them:

"I am the living bread which came down from Heaven: if any man eat of this bread, he shall live forever: and the bread that I will give is my flesh, which I will give for the life of the world. Verily, verily I say to you, Except you eat the flesh of the Son of Man, and drink His blood, you

have no life in you. He that eats My flesh and drinks My blood, dwells in Me and I in him." (John 6:51,53,56)

Here is yet another reference to both blood and flesh. There is no indication anywhere in all of Scripture that God condones either cannibalism, or the drinking of blood. Indeed, God specifically prohibits the drinking of blood (Genesis 9:4; Leviticus 11:10-12), and says that He will not hear the cry for help of those who eat the flesh of His people. (Micah 3:1-4) It is clear that the words of Jesus are metaphorical. Sin and death consume the flesh of mankind. However, those who partake of Jesus, by way of communion with Him, gain life everlasting.

Jesus was making clear that, under the Torah, if anyone drank blood they would be cut off. However, because He is the True Life, His blood resurrects and offers Eternal Life. Thus, He was portraying Himself as the True Sacrifice, the Sacrifice which could only be revealed once the first tabernacles, the Tabernacle of Moses and the Temple of Solomon, were no longer standing. His tabernacle was the tabernacle not made with hands. Therefore, it was the more perfect tabernacle. (Hebrews 9:8-22)

As clear as His words seem to us today, many of those who claimed to be disciples of Jesus "went back and walked with Him no more." (John 6:66) This was a difficult teaching for the Jews to hear, because they were steeped in tradition, and the Torah. Ironically, it was precisely because of their traditions, and because of the teachings of the Torah, that Jesus spoke to them in this manner.

Many things in the Old Testament are types and shadows of things to come. And it is in the construction of the Tabernacle of Moses that we see repeated types and shadows of Christ.

The Mercy Seat was constructed of pure gold and was placed upon the top of the Ark of the Covenant. Inside the Ark were the two tablets of stone on which were written the Ten Commandments. God met with the children of Israel only in the Holy of Holies, and only through the High Priest. He communicated with the High Priest "from above the Mercy Seat, from between the two cherubim which are upon the Ark of the testimony." (Exodus 25:17-22)

The Mercy Seat was made of one piece of gold, but had three figures: two cherubim and a blood-stained mercy seat. One cherub represented God the Father, one represented God the Holy Spirit, and in the middle, the blood-stained mercy seat represented Christ. Romans 3:25 tells us that Jesus was "a propitiation, through faith in His blood, to declare His righteousness for the remission of sins that are past, through the forbearance of God." The Greek word used in this passage for "propitiation" is the same Greek word used in Hebrews 9:5 and translated there as "mercy seat."

We are also told that the Shepherd of Israel dwells between the cherubim (Psalm 80:1), and that the Lord reigns and sits between the cherubim (Psalm 99:1). And it was cherubim who were assigned to guard the Tree of Life with flaming swords when man was cast out of the Garden of Eden because of sin. (Genesis 3:21-24) Thus, cherubim are associated with the judgment of sin.

The triune construction of the Mercy Seat symbolized the Holy Trinity.

The fact that it was fashioned from one piece of gold represented the unity, the Oneness, of the Godhead. This is the essence of the *Shema* of Israel, "Hear O Israel: the Lord our God is one Lord." (Deuteronomy 6:4) It also foreshadowed the unity of both Jew and Gentile, through the blood sacrifice of Jesus, into One New Man, the habitation of God. (Ephesians 2:11-22; 1Corinthians 3:16)

It is in the Tabernacle of Moses that we see the blending of judgment *and* mercy.

The grate on the Brazen Altar, which is a type and shadow of the Cross, where the burnt offerings, the sin offerings, and the trespass offerings were made, was the place of God's Judgment. It was here that the sin of the entire nation of Israel was judged and atoned for by the substitute sacrifices. And when the blood was brought to, and placed upon, the Mercy Seat, the whole nation was reconciled to God. (Leviticus 16) To remove the Mercy Seat and look upon the Ten Commandments, the Law, without the covering of blood meant instant death. (1Samuel 6:19-20)

To reject the sacrificial blood is to reject the Spirit of Life. (Romans 8:2)

This was the Judgmental aspect of God.

On the other hand, it is significant that the Mercy Seat was a "seat."

It is the only seat in the entire Tabernacle.

The priests *stood* daily ministering and offering sacrifices, but it was Christ Who, once He had offered His blood as a single sacrifice for sins forever, *sat* down on the right hand of God. (Hebrews 10:11-12) That Christ sat down is significant of both entering into His rest (Hebrews 4:8-10), and His finished work on the Cross. (Isaiah 16:5; John 19:30) Thus, to embrace the blood is to receive the restoration of all things. (Revelation 5:8-10)

The Mercy Seat was also the place above which the Glory of God manifested. It was above the Mercy Seat, between the cherubim, where God spoke in an audible voice. (Exodus 29:42, 30:6,36; Numbers 7:89) The Jews refer to the visible manifestation of His Glory as the *Shekinah*, which literally means "One who dwells." The visible Glory residing over the Ark was so strong that Moses literally addressed the Ark as "Lord." (Numbers 10:35-36)

If the Mercy Seat was the type and shadow of the Glory to come, then it is in the person of Jesus that we see the fulfillment of that type and shadow, the indwelling Manifest Presence of God.

Immanuel.

God in us.

God with us.

Moses had this revelation. He cried out to God until He saw the Glory. If we are as earnest, and as sincere, as Moses we too will see the Glory of God in the face of Jesus. (2Corinthians 4:6) This is why Jesus is called the "Brightness of His Glory, and the express image of His Person." (Hebrews 1:3) It is also why He is called "the Lord of Glory." (1Corinthians 2:8) One day, His Glory will light the entire earth. (Revelation 18:1)

All of this was made possible by the shedding of His Precious Blood.

Initially, God instituted *Pesach*, the Passover, saying, "When I see the blood, I will pass over you." (Exodus 12:13) He then provided a way for the Jews to receive atonement for sin in the shedding of the blood of animals. But it is in the final sacrifice, the shedding of the blood of Jesus that God's promise to Israel, and to those of us who believe on Him, is fulfilled.

It is by the shedding of His Precious Blood that we are reconciled to Him, and that the curse brought upon mankind by Adam and Eve's transgression is forever cancelled.

Printed in the United States
77747LV00004BA/1-192